LETTERS OF RECOMMENDATION

I've found Peter's history and chronicles refreshing, as they were instructive. I've learned a lot from the probity, accountability, and integrity he exhibited during his public career and during my personal experience with him in Burundi, when he adhered to strict principles based on his personal relationship with Christ. I strongly recommend his writings to the body of Christ.

Archbishop Otis Vandyke Noah Sr. Pastor of MRCCI, Minneapolis, MN 55412

Archbishop Dr. Vandyke Noah's career accomplishments include training over 300 pastors and ministers, empowering them to direct churches. He is a writer and author, and his books have been distributed worldwide. He also serves as a radio host and the executive producer of Solution Time Radio. Archbishop Dr. Vandyke Noah holds a number of positions: board member of Africa for Israel, which is an organization that supports the nation of Israel; board member and chaplain for New Enterprise Holdings; president of the Global Administrative Counsel of MRCCI worldwide; Middle Eastern coordinator for Morris Cerullo Ministries from 1994-2000; president and CEO of Vandyke Noah Ministries; and founder and bishop of Miracle Redemption Christian Center Worldwide.

Born on November 14, 1965, in Accra, Ghana, Archbishop Vandyke Noah obtained a B.A. in Theology from King of Kings College in Jerusalem, Israel, in 1994. He attended Advanced Theology/Hebrew Interpretation at Jerusalem University in Israel and was awarded an honorary Ph.D. in Theology from

Cosmopolitan University in the USA. He married Ruby on March 26, 1994, and they have one child. In his spare time Archbishop Vandyke Noah enjoys reading, walking, and jogging.

Everything in life happens for the eventual fulfillment of God's purpose and His Holy Kingdom. I have always believed this! And it is not by chance that Peter Idusogie came into my life at the time and the place he did. As someone who loves the Lord but has often felt like a wanderer in a desolate, barren land, Peter came into my life like a deep, cool well of refreshing water for my soul. Peter is a fierce and determined man of faith, and he became an instant inspiration to me as a brother in Christ. Every week I looked forward to hearing his short sermonettes in the small confines of my office, as the Word of God often poured from his lips like a nurturing spring of encouragement! When Peter prays, the presence of God is immediately palpable to His children, and as we frequently fellowshipped in the Lord, it became more and more apparent that Peter would not be in the car business for long.

When Peter approached me to write a short bio for him for his book, I was honored. I have always loved the Lord, and while I have regretfully been a sinner, I have also been redeemed by the grace and mercy of our Lord and Savior, Jesus Christ. With that said, I've also always tried to love people as God loves me and to give back in whatever capacity I could. Unfortunately, for most of my life, I've often found myself tied to the world in more ways then I'd like, having chosen a career as a finance director for one of the world's largest Mercedes Benz dealers. The opportunities for ministry have been few and far between, but as I grew closer to Peter, I began to be inspired by the Lord, and I have since started a salsa company with another good friend of mine as a means of ministry and reaching those in need. We have already tasted God's blessing in the year we have been in business by hosting fundraisers for a few non-profits and by raising money for one of the largest dog rescues in Oklahoma, and a part of our success can no doubt be attributed to Peter's prayers.

While I feel I may fall short in my testimony to Peter, I know that his testimony for the Lord will yield tremendous fruit. He is not only well versed in God's Word, but Peter also sees the shortcomings of this world in which we live, and his discernment has given him great insight into the wickedness of this generation, especially in the political scene. While I have not yet had the privilege to read his book, I am greatly anticipating being edified by what he has to say. We are indeed at a crossroads globally, with moral relativism ruling the day, and a voice like Peter's needs to be heard! Peter has a calling for the Lord, for the truth! And I cannot wait to see how the Lord uses him.

In Christ Alone,
Damon Paul Clay
Financial Director
Mercedes Benz Dallas-Park Place Motorcars
Dallas, TX 75209

Damon Paul Clay works as a financial director for Park Place Motors, Mercedes Benz Dallas. Park Place Motors is recognized as one of the top 100 companies to work for in the Dallas/Fort Worth area. Mercedes Benz Dallas is in one of the wealthiest suburbs in Dallas and is one of the top five Mercedes Benz stores in the United States.

I am writing to attest to the character of Peter Idusogie, whom I have known for approximately seven years. I have had the opportunity to hear and see him interact with people in various ministry and personal situations. Peter is a minister of the gospel of Jesus Christ, a prayer warrior with a Kingdom mindset. He has a strong gift of dreams and visions. He has a heart for the nations and the Church to have a reverential fear of the Lord.

Peter is an excellent role model for men seeking a more active and rewarding relationship with our Savior, Jesus Christ. He is loved and respected by his peers. Peter is doctrinally sound and balanced. His teaching is always Bible-centered, and he treats the Word of God with great love and respect. Whether speaking to believers or unbelievers, his presentation is always passionate, biblical, and compelling. In addition, his winsome personality always engages his audience.

Peter is an ardent soul-winner, and he has tremendous skill with public speaking. He is an excellent communicator and a brilliant writer. Because of his background in politics, he understands the heartbeat of the Church, the government, and the intricacies of ministry.

It has been my honor to know and be friends with Peter and his lovely wife, Juanita, and I am confident that he has the experience, character, and personality necessary to make an outstanding author.

I have been pleased to witness Peter's spiritual growth over time, and I look forward to seeing it blossom further. I respect him as a person of moral and godly character. I believe the Lord will use him greatly throughout his ministry. It is my pleasure to recommend Peter Idusogie.

Sincerely,
Felicia Graves
Dallas, TX 75360

Felicia Graves is an accomplished deliverance minister of the gospel of Jesus Christ. She is gifted with knowledge of the Word and is also an ordained prophet and minister of the gospel. She has traveled to different parts of the country as an invited guest, preaching about the importance of using the Word of God as a sword to ward off the devil and his growing works of darkness in the world. She is a prolific teacher who explains how the saints of today can equip themselves by reading what the Bible teaches, which will help them withstand the works of the devil. She believes the Bible is unique among all other religious books, in the sense that it was inspired by the Holy Spirit and nearly all of its predictions have come to pass. Felicia currently runs a prayer room ministry in Dallas, Texas.

This book by Peter Idusogie will be one of the most compelling books of The Ordination of America By God Himself! Reading this timely material will open your eyes about the works of Satan. Indeed, this book portrays the devil's plot to destroy our sacred country by spreading the seed of division among brethren and fellow citizens. The "bad fruit" is very much in our midst today. Also, this book will expose the evil perpetuated by the radicals who, in their ignorance or lack of understanding of our nation's history, seek to unravel the American way of life, which was originally founded on the principles of God. Enjoy this book! It will excite and ignite your faith, helping you be a steadfast Christian and a better, prouder American.

Rev. Richard W Hayes
Power and Life Church Ministries
Dallas, TX 75217

Rev. Hayes is recognized for using God's power to heal the sick, cast out devils, and, most importantly, bring souls to Christ. Rev. Richard W. Hayes is the son of Rev. Alton L. Hayes, who was known as the youngest man in the Voice of Healing movement. Voice of Healing published its own worldwide magazine, featuring nationally-known evangelists such as A. A. Allen, Jack Coe, William Branham, W. V. Grant Sr., T. L. Osborne, and more. During the dynamic miracle years of the 50s and 60s, his campaign manager was Gordon Lindsey from Christ for the Nations.

"Big Bro" is what I call this fine gentleman with a good heart and immense kindness. God's call on his life has been evident since he was a young lad, when he went down on bended knees to pray for God to forgive the person who ransacked his closet. Brother Peter's revelation dreams are accurate, but his scriptural expositions are even more phenomenal.

His life is filled with many mind-blowing testimonies on the faithfulness of God, who has granted him victory every step of the way on this battlefield of life.

Oghogho Maria Mudasiru

Dr. Oghogho Maria Mudasiru is a graduate from Rhema Bible College in Abuja. She is a successful entrepreneur, a real estate investor, and, above all, a philanthropist of the highest order. Her acts of benevolence to the less fortunate in Africa, including underwriting college tuitions for some of the children in Africa and other ministries, is worthy of adoration and admiration.

AMERICA
— ORDAINED BY —
GOD

Perilous Times Ahead

PETER I. IDUSOGIE

This book is dedicated to the true saints of God, on a global level, who have been interceding for America through prayer and fasting. They are crying out to God to be patient with America, praying that the American people, along with the rest of the world, will heed the call of wisdom at the city gates and in the town square. They are praying that people will be reconciled with God and one another by destroying the spirit of division, anger, bitterness, chaos, wickedness, pride, vengeance, deception, murder, and rebellion against God's Word and divine authority, which originated in the pit of hell itself.

CONTENTS

ACKNOWLEDGMENTS

I want to express my sincere gratitude to my wife, Juanita, who has been a tireless supporter and a helping hand during every project I have undertaken for the fulfillment of my God-given destiny. This book, and others to come, is long overdue. Finally, my deepest appreciation to the Almighty God for being patient and ever so gentle with me. He used the Holy Spirit to encourage me to move forward and embark on those things that were already written about me in heaven. Above all, He gave me the time and space to write this book. Remember the Lord's prayer: "...Thy will be done in earth, as it is in heaven" (Mt 6:10 KJV). Thank you, Elohim Chayim, for there is no God like you. Yes indeed, there is no God like Jehovah. Mighty is our God, ruler of everything.

A Prayer for the Reader

Heavenly Father, I come before You in the name of Your Son, Jesus Christ. Empower me to absorb and understand what it is You want me to glean from this book. Let the Word of God that is written in this book be uplifting, instructive, corrective, and nourishing to my soul. Yes, Lord, I want a deeper walk with You that is not obligatory or religious but desirable and loving. Enable me to understand Your unfailing love for me, which can be life-transforming and can have great eternal rewards. To You be all the honor, glory, power, majesty, and riches forever and ever. Amen.

INTRODUCTION

On April 2, 2020, at the height of the global Coronavirus outbreak, I received a phone call after returning home from work. The phone call was from the director of new cars, along with one of the three senior managers at Park Place Motorcars, Mercedes Benz Dallas. I was gainfully employed as an experienced sales manager at one of the top five Mercedes stores in the country. They informed me during the conference call that I had been laid off, along with 450 others, due to the lockdown caused by the Coronavirus outbreak that started in Wuhan, China. Stunned by what I had heard, I asked them to repeat what they said. "You are being laid off," they told me again. There was a severance package being mailed to me. A great sense of calm and peace came over me after the phone call. There was absolutely no nervousness, worry, concern, or fear. Instead, the reassuring presence of the Spirit of God overwhelmed me.

It is written: "You will keep in perfect *and* constant peace *the one* whose mind is steadfast [that is, committed and focused on You—in both inclination and character], Because he trusts *and* takes refuge in You [with hope and confident expectation]" (Is 26:3 AMP).

What I was perceiving in my heart were these words: "They did not lay you off; I did. I am giving you yet another opportunity to enter into those things that are written about you in heaven."

"I get it, Lord," was my response. After that acknowledgment a sense of confidence was immediately established within me. With more time on my hands, I began to daily read the Scriptures in greater detail than I usually did. I had developed a habit over the years of reading the Bible every day, no matter how busy or tired I was. I certainly did not do this for religious reasons; I did it because I had come to understand with time that the Bible is the most powerful book ever written, and I enjoyed meditating on the Word of God. I drew this conclusion based on prophesies made in the Bible and the prophesies that had already been fulfilled. Even if you are not a Christian or a follower of Jesus Christ, if you read something like the book of Proverbs in the Bible—written in large part by King Solomon, the son of the giant killer in Israel—you will gain wisdom. There are great rewards that come to anyone who reads the Bible with understanding, regardless of the person's religion or faith, and especially with the help of the Holy Spirit.

After a week of being laid off, I turned to the book of Revelation, the last book in the Bible, to read it all over again. I cannot count how many times I have read the book of Revelation, but it still remains one of the most fascinating books in the Bible, and I believe we are the generation that will literally experience some of the things that are yet to come. I believe we will see events unfold in our midst, depending on whether we are raptured before the end times begin. We may witness the beginning of the end times while being spared by God from the fiery trials others will face. The other scenario is that those who are truly reborn and have a loving relationship with the Heavenly Father through His Son, Jesus Christ, will depart from the earth just after the antichrist assumes global authority. There is a large debate within the Christian community over which one will take place first, and it does not bother me at all. Time will eventually tell which of these scenarios is God's perfect will. I had barely gone past the first chapter in the book of Revelation when the Spirit of God began to move me to write a book about His mighty hand in the affairs of America. The Spirit of God wanted me to include insight from the first three chapters of the book of Revelation. God has a reward for each person who overcomes diverse temptations and trials that have come upon the earth to test allegiance to Christ, the Messiah, and the Savior of the world.

I will also be drawing excerpts from the entire Bible to underscore the Spirit of God's purpose in this book. God has a solemn message for all of us, especially those of us who identify with Jesus Christ and are reborn. No other nation in the last two centuries has experienced the kind of blessings and prosperity the United States of America has experienced. Apart from Israel and other ancient empires, God singled out the United States to display His glory on the earth in our time and age, and yet this truth is still missing in the hearts of millions of Americans. Other nations cannot understand why America has been single-handedly responsible for many of the social, economic, scientific, technological, agricultural, and medical breakthroughs the whole world has benefited from. I am sent to remind this generation that America's inherent greatness and its history of accomplishments came only from the Almighty God, lest any American should boast. The people who question whether this country's founding fathers had a covenant with God have either never traveled out of the United States or are unaware of how America stands out as a beacon of hope among the community of nations, even when, for various reasons, the world may not like the current president in the White House. One of these reasons is that some of things our president has said were not properly thought through, and another reason is that many people wanted a woman as president, which did not happen. So it did not matter which man became president; they were going to hate that person anyway. Lastly, people dislike him because he has been, to a large extent, unfairly portrayed by the media in very negative terms, unlike any other president since our independence. And yes, we are in a different era from times past, and plainspoken truth has been replaced with masking the truth in order to not offend others. Nevertheless, the United States of America continues to impact and influence how the peoples of this world live their lives, and it will continue to do so for the foreseeable future.

The impact of this nation on the lives of the people of the world is monumental and mind-boggling. It would take hundreds of books to describe America's influence on the world. Just take social media as an example. It was invented in the U.S., and the whole world now enjoys it. We turned sports into an entertainment industry, and thousands were enriched by it after we built multi-million-dollar stadiums for various sports. As if this weren't enough, video games were introduced for children and adults so they could have virtual realities. Our products and services have touched every nation on Earth. Even though there are things we no longer manufacture or make due to global commerce and outsourcing of the manufacturing to China, Vietnam, and India, the technology and the blueprints of what is manufactured in those countries indeed came from our homeland, the United States of America.

Unfortunately, some of these blessing upon our country have become idols in our hearts. This is exactly what brings down nations that God has raised up, as the God of Abraham, Isaac, and Jacob is a jealous God. An idol is anything you are obsessed with and spend a considerable amount of time with—more than you allot to your Heavenly Father. Now, we all have this problem to some extent, but some of us are really out of control. You know when you have an idol in your heart. Having an idol can also mean worshiping nonliving materials, like stones people put around their necks. They give them names and say they protect them. These are idols, and there are spiritual consequences that will manifest physically and that will unfortunately affect your children's children, all the way to the third and fourth generations, as there will be problems and trials in their lives that they will face because of God's anger.

America today is departing from godliness and good living. The consequences are obvious, as separation from God always brings an inevitable curse on the whole nation. Powerful evidence of this curse is the spirit of division that now pervades the whole country. We look at the reasons why, and we are quick to point fingers at each other. Republicans against Democrats. Socialists and anarchists against what they perceive is a corrupt capitalist system with too many "have nots." They are the powerful billionaires who have gained tremendous wealth from the capitalist system, and yet they want to reestablish a new economic system and a single world government, thinking it will solve our problems, but their motives are evil and not of God at all. Even though the Bible has warned us, they will eventually succeed, and they will curtail our freedoms, oppress us, and severely persecute the Christians. Yet the underlying reason for all of this is spiritual. It has been a long time coming. Make no mistake about this: Jesus also spoke about this division we are witnessing in the world today. Yet God longs to have real fellowship with all Americans who are willing to allow Him to enter into their hearts through His Son. God will heal your wounds, emotions, pains, and hurts, and through His Holy Spirit, He will settle the most pressing needs of your entire being. God will also shield you from the terrible times that are to befall the earth very soon. This is the time to stop playing footsie in your relationship with God. This is what Jesus says to you and me.

It is written: "Here I am! I stand at the door and knock. If anyone hears my voice and opens the door, I will come in and eat with that person, and they with me" (Rv 3:20 NIV).

Notice that Jesus did not say, "if you are a Christian," because not all people who identify themselves as Christians are going to make it to heaven. Jesus did not say, "if you are baptized," although doing this is also great. He is knocking on the door of your heart right now. His voice is His Word, and you have just read His Word. God wants to do something even greater than what America has accomplished since it gained its independence from Great Britain. God wants to give every American an opportunity to be reborn, which is the requirement for you to make it to heaven when you leave this earth; otherwise you will be separated from Him for eternity. Eternity is life without end, so this is no small matter. To the American people, God says, "'I have loved you with an everlasting love...'" (Jer 31:3 NIV). Joshua said, "'...destroy the idols among you, and turn your hearts to the Lord, the God of Israel" (Jo 24:23 NLV). There are indeed wonderful and amazing rewards that will last for eternity for those who overcome and do not abandon their sworn fidelity to the Father through His Son, Jesus Christ, known as Yeshua in Hebrew. To those who have no relationship with God through His Son, Jesus Christ, God wants you to embrace the truth, which is that Jesus was sent to this world to save you. All you have to do is believe in your heart and confess to yourself that Jesus is the true Son of God, and He came to die for your sins so that you can be reconciled with the Father in heaven. He wants you to do this before it is too late. He wants you to know that death can come knocking at the door anytime, usually when you least expect it to happen.

Remember that Kobe Bryant, Whitney Houston, Prince, and Michael Jackson didn't have a clue when their last breath on Earth would come to pass. It happened suddenly, without notice. It was not caused by long bout of illness, and it wasn't suicide. Again, death came without notice. It doesn't matter how great their funerals or eulogies were; those things could not alter their destinations once they had their last breath on Earth. Some religions tell you that you will go to purgatory if you are not that bad. That is not true. It is unbiblical, and Jesus never, ever said that. Jesus spoke more about hell and heaven than any preacher who

xxii

walked the earth in His time, because He created them. To the main press, remember Tim Russert of *Meet the Press* on NBC. He was one of my favorite TV news anchormen, and he died suddenly nearly twelve years ago. It was a sad day for American women and men in the news industry. He had just returned from a vacation with his family in Italy and was getting ready to prepare for his Sunday show, but he collapsed and died.

The Holy Spirit doesn't want the American people, and the rest of the world, to listen to the lies that there is no heaven or hell. Nothing could be further from the truth. Do not listen to the naysayers who question and discount life after death. It is the sophisticated work of the spirit of the antichrist to deceive the world. Although the person who will eventually carry that title has not yet been revealed, his spirit is hard at work deceiving many people. Remember, naysayers did the same thing to Noah, making fun of him and saying that it hadn't rained for 150 years. Then the rain came, and the mockers all perished when God opened the fountains of the deep and the clouds poured down rain. Search the Scriptures for yourself rather than allow yourself to be deceived; otherwise you will be faced with incalculable consequences that will last for eternity—forever and forever. You know what is so funny? Noah was able to convince the baboons, tigers, and goats, who usually act dumb and are stubborn, but no human being made it into the ark apart from Noah's immediate family. And that was sad. My prayer is that the deception sweeping the country, especially among our youth, will not foster in their hearts a stubborn spirit worse than Noah's generation. In Jesus' name. Amen!

Today, millions of Americans are facing one crisis after another, from economic issues to health issues to utter confusion about what they want to do with their individual lives. Some have contemplated suicide. To those of you who are facing a crisis beyond your ability to cope with or handle, try Christ Jesus before you take your life. Jesus is the Son of God, and His loving kindness toward you is better than life itself. It will be impossible to discover love from God through His Son if you prematurely take your life. Seek help and counsel from a loved one if you are struggling to subdue the voice of Satan when he tells you to kill yourself.

I am aware that the suicide rate has risen in states that have been hit hard by Covid-19. As I began to write this book, it was reported in the news that California has had a higher increase in suicide attempts in one month than in the entirety of last year. Yes, it is true that life has its battles and that life is not a party parlor but a race to the finish line. Maybe life has been rough since you were born, and you have not seen the light at the end of the tunnel. You may be suffering from depression, or maybe you are currently facing insurmountable difficulties, such as excruciating physical pain or even emotional pain and distress. You may have lost a loved one or your job because of Covid-19. God wants you to know that He is fully aware of your circumstances and cares for you immensely. He loves you. The voice telling you to take your life may be diagnosed as a mental problem, but the spirit behind that mental problem is none other than Satan, who has come to take you out before your time because he senses that God is seeking to glorify His name in your life and current predicament.

God is known all over the world to move powerfully in difficult circumstances. He is not only the God of the suddenly; He is also the God of the midnight hour. Consider the immense suffering of the poor in Haiti, the refugee camps in war-stricken Syria and Lebanon, and the poverty-stricken little children in the developing parts of the world, many of whom are surviving on barely one meal a day. If you feel there is no point in living, consider donating your time to a worthy cause, and you will find meaning in your life. If you take your life, you will never discover your purpose. Turn your heart toward others. Become a helping hand rather than focusing on your temporary predicament. God can change your circumstances in the twinkling of an eye if you will only dare to trust Him. He alone knows the end from the beginning and the beginning from the end.

It is written: "So we don't look at the troubles we can see now; rather, we fix our gaze on things that cannot be seen. For the things we see now will soon be gone, but the things we cannot see will last forever" (2 Cor 4:18 NLT).

Chapter 1

ABSOLUTE GREATNESS

"He makes nations great, and he destroys them; he enlarges nations, and leads them away" (Jb 12:23 ESV).

My fellow Americans and people of the entire earth, may the Lord bless you. May the Lord keep you. May the Lord shine His face on you, and may He be gracious to you. May the Lord lift up His countenance to you, and may the Lord grant you His shalom, His peace.

Now read carefully. Hear this, America and the peoples of the world: It is the one true God—the God of Abraham, Isaac, Jacob of Israel—who makes nations great. He is also the one who makes people great. He is also the one who punishes nations when they depart from His ways and reject Him after He has made them great. After all, He is known as Quana, a jealous God. God does this to humble those nations once more, so that they may remember He is the one who gives the power to create wealth and that He may establish His covenant with them.

God is the one who protects individuals from global pandemics that come upon other people or nations. There are powerful examples of this truth in the Bible. It is not based on whether you go to church or whether you are a pastor, a minister, an Iman, a rabbi, a Hindu high priest, or a member of a Christian clergy. Let us not forget that

1

even Satan and his agents, along with the disobedient, visit churches from time to time.

There are always some who remain immune to the diverse trials that come on the earth, both in the past and in the future. God wants all people to enter into this special protection reserved exclusively for those who have a loving relationship with God through His Son, Jesus Christ. These are the ones who obey Him, even if it makes them unpopular or hated in the world we live in today. It doesn't mean these people don't face persecution or sickness, but He promises to see them through it. Remember what it says in the word of God: "God has spoken once, Twice I have heard this: That power *belongs* to God" (Ps 62:11 NKJV). God protects those who have a reverent fear of Him and worship Him with their obedience. Obedience to God is a form of worship. Otherwise you are just flattering Him, and He knows that, too. There is a pastor in Africa who, according to Time Magazine, is regarded as one of the fifty most important and most influential people in the world. He has not gotten sick since he became the head of Redeem Christian Church of God. He says God promised to take sickness away from him. He lives in Africa, where there are diverse kinds of diseases, but he is also a globetrotter because he is sought after by kings of nations and ordinary men on the streets. My wife and I have never been troubled by this pandemic. Our confidence is assured, and we are secure in the Lord. We know we are not the only ones, as there are many of us who have been blessed with this supernatural protection, and we rejoice in the Lord and the power of His might. We shall not fear the next one, which is expected to come in 2021.

God loves America, and He ordained its existence. God wants to protect the territory where He has invested a tremendous amount of his blessings— more than any other modern nation today. God's wisdom, wealth, riches, honor, power, and expression of His love have been poured into

2

America since it gained its independence from Great Britain, where I was born. Those of us who were not originally born in the United States but are citizens of this amazing nation know how much God has blessed America. We know He loves America. It is the United States, after all, that has spread the gospel through missionaries and television to all the earth. Since you cannot outgive God, our Heavenly Father knows how to reward nations that engage in this exercise and are not ashamed to identify with Him. Unfortunately, in the quest for more freedom, the desires of America have gravitated incrementally but steadily toward wanting to be free from God's principles and commandments. We have started to view God's boundaries as impediments to living a lifestyle that we want, even if it is outside God's will.

It is written: "They remembered that God was their Rock, that God Most High was their Redeemer. But then they would flatter him with their mouths, lying to him with their tongues; their hearts were not loyal to him..." (Ps 78:35-37 NIV).

Great nations have been recognized on the world stage for their military might and the expansion of territories they occupied. These empires and kingdoms eventually grew to become epicenters of trade and commerce at the height of their reign. To a large extent, this was also dependent on how ambitious the emperor or king was. Equally important, the rise or fall of a nation was dependent on how much favor they had with God. Because God is a sovereign King, it was not uncommon for Him to show favor to world leaders who did not even worship Him but still acknowledged His great power. For example, the Bible tells us in the book of Genesis that Nimrod was a mighty hunter before God. He was a warrior-like leader who was a pagan and worshiped idols, lifeless gods. Yet he was a skilled battlefield tactician, and God respected him because it was God who made him what he became known for. In fact, the HMS Navy (the British royal navy) has given six of their warships the name

Nimrod. They know this name came from the Bible, so I really can't understand how people today still question the authenticity and accuracy of the Bible.

Another king of ancient times who did not worship God but respected Him was King Cyrus. The Bible tells us how King Cyrus, even though he did not know God, was highly favored by God, and God helped King Cyrus subdue his enemies. In return, King Cyrus was used by God to help the Jews return to Israel and rebuild their temple after they were held captive and exiled to Babylon by King Nebuchadnezzar. King Cyrus even went so far as to ask his treasury secretary to give the Jews whatever they needed to make the trip back to Israel. On the other hand, there were other leaders and nations who were blessed by God because they were true worshipers of the great God of heaven and Earth. One such person was Abraham. God called Abraham His friend. Another important personality was Joseph, who became the first Hebrew to be a vice president of a foreign nation, and he had vast powers to govern that nation. This took place more than 5,000 years ago. During that period Egypt was the most powerful nation on the planet.

It is also true that through the great power of God, a young shepherd boy who was relegated to keeping sheep for his small family business in animal husbandry, later known as King David, arose from obscurity to become a giant killer, a skilled warrior, and a successful king. Prior to that accomplishment, while in the wilderness keeping sheep, he mastered poetry by authoring most of what is called the book of Psalms in the Bible—prayers of worship, thanksgiving, repentance, and requests for help. He also made sweet melodies in praise of the living God, Elohim Chayim. So pleased was the Almighty God with this young fellow, He called David "a man after His own heart." God also empowered David to become the king of Israel and enabled him to conquer and occupy a prime and beautiful land.

4

Even to this day, hour, minute, and second, this land God Almighty gave King David is the most disputed real estate territory on the face of the earth, and that is Jerusalem. This never belonged to the Palestinians of today or the Israelites of the past. It belonged to the Jebusites. No descendants of the Jebusites exist on Earth today, and God gave David the military tactics to invade and take it over. The Jebusites were doing things that were detestable to God, including worshiped a false god, so God gave that land over to someone who loved and worshiped Him. In His infinite wisdom God also made a vow through His prophets, on more than one occasion, that His Son, Jesus Christ, would come from the lineage of David when He was born. We know that on the account of one or two witnesses, the Word of God was established.

It is written: "'Your house (royal dynasty) and your kingdom will endure forever before Me; your throne will be established forever'" (2 Sm 7:16 AMP). It is written: "'Behold (listen closely), the days are coming,' says the LORD, 'When I will raise up for David a righteous Branch; And He will reign as King and act wisely And will do [those things that accomplish] justice and righteousness in the land. In His Days Judah will be saved, And Israel will dwell safely; Now this is His name by which He will be called; "The LORD Our Righteousness"'" (Jer 23:5-6 AMP).

So David became king of Judah, and later of Jerusalem (now part of Israel), after defeating the Jebusites, who were the original inhabitants of Jerusalem. King David ruled a swarth of territory known as Israel, along with other territories he conquered. Right before his death he handed over his reign to his son Solomon, known as Solomon the wise man, who was later crowned as king of Israel. Solomon was visited by God in his dream, and God promised to make him great fabulously wealthy because he asked for wisdom to rule his people rather than money. The fulfillment of that promise allowed Solomon to be the wisest man on the earth in his time, and he was the wealthiest man who will ever occupy the earth. Israel under King Solomon had more gold and precious metals than any modern nation has today. He did not need a federal reserve system to print paper money. Solomon ended up departing temporarily from the things of God and started worshiping other gods. Does this sound familiar? This caused his kingdom to be divided, and Solomon lost the prestige and clout he had when he worshiped the one true God.

It is written: "God gave Solomon wisdom and very great insight, and a breadth of understanding as measureless as the sand on the seashore. Solomon's wisdom was greater than the wisdom of all the people of the East, and greater than all the wisdom of Egypt. He was wiser than anyone else… And his fame spread to all the surrounding nations. He spoke three thousand proverbs and his songs numbered a thousand and five. He spoke about plant life, from the cedar of Lebanon to the hyssop that grows out of walls. He also spoke about animals and birds, reptiles and fish. From all nations people came to listen to Solomon's wisdom, sent by all the kings of the world, who had heard of his wisdom" (1 Kgs 4:29-34 NIV). Other versions say that every nation on Earth sent ambassadors to Israel so they could learn something from Solomon, and then they would come back to report what they had learned.

In summary, for several thousands of years, empires and kingdoms have emerged to seize the center stage in the world, only to be replaced by another nation led by a more ambitious and determined leaders, with world domination so often on their minds. Yet, at the end of the day, each of these nations and their leaders were only tools in the hands of God, used to carry out His plans for the earth. It has always been about the sovereignty of God, who already knows the choices of man and thus acts accordingly. Indeed, it is God who makes nations and their leaders great. The

Bible reminds us, "The Lord is a man of war: the Lord is his name" (Ex 15:3 KJV).

How can we forget the world leaders who had the word "Great" attached to their names? King Cyrus the Great. Alexander the Great, who ruled and conquered literally almost the whole world from 336 BC to 323 BC. Julius Caesar, who was head of the Roman Empire, was considered an extraordinarily great leader. Peter the Great, who was from Russia and ruled from 1682 to 1725. Each left an indelible mark on the pages of history. These leaders were noted for their military conquests, the acquisition of more territories through successful wars and military campaigns. Yes, some of these leaders were oppressive, and others were noted for their introduction of much-needed reforms to alleviate the suffering of the poor and less privileged.

Major universities and academic institutions of higher learning have studied these ancient empires and kingdoms. It would be unthinkable to undertake a world history course without doing a case study on the Russian Revolution, the French Revolution, the rise of Alexander the Great, and the Napoleonic Wars. Today, you can watch the history channel on cable TV, or even a movie on Netflix, to learn about the fall and rise of these nations. The top military colleges of the world study their war tactics. Each of these institutions— whether they are academic universities or military universities, such as West Point in the U.S. or Sandhurst in England— tries to learn lessons from the armies and navies of these great nations of the past, hoping those lessons can be applied to the wars that will be fought in the future.

Great Britain was the last known modern-day empire that our generation can relate to, other than the ancient Greek or Persian empires. This is because it wasn't that long ago that the British Empire ruled as an occupying force longer than any other known empire. Also, unlike any other country on Earth, Great Britain controlled and occupied more than half of the territories on the earth. This was a remarkable accomplishment for an island nation in Western Europe that had less than eight million people in the 17th century. Today, although no longer a great empire, the majestic trappings and assets of the British monarchy are legendary and still intact. The royal family of Great Britain today is headed by Her Majesty and Royal Highness, Queen Elizabeth II. Despite the seismic change from the past in what it controls and owns, the British monarchy is still the most powerful and famous royal family in the world, and they are a huge revenue generator for the British tourist industry and the British economy. In addition, many believe the powerful Federal Reserve Bank in the United States is still run by eight families who are based in the United Kingdom. It is interesting to note that great nations of the past have always been headed by a king, emperor, or a queen until a nation like America came about and chose to become a constitutional republic rather than subscribe to the governing style of its former colonial ruler, England.

I thank God for America. God has truly blessed the American people and, as a result, blessed America. Its citizens are truly a remarkable group of people whose origins today comprise of nations that span the entire globe. Together, they have not only transformed America into a mighty nation before God, but they have also transformed the world. Without a doubt, America has had its challenges and shortcomings, and not everything has been hunky-dory since it gained its independence from Great Britain. It is written: "Daniel spake and said, I saw in my vision by night, and, behold, the four winds of the heaven strove upon the great sea. And four great beasts came up from the sea, diverse one from another. The first was like a lion, and had eagle's wings: I beheld till the wings thereof were plucked, and it was lifted up from the earth, and made stand upon the feet as a man, and a man's heart was given to it" (Dn 7:2-4 KJV).

Friends, many have erroneously attributed this Scripture to reference the reign of King Nebuchadnezzar. On the contrary, a close observation shows that the Scripture was making a clear reference to the United States of America. You see, the symbol for Great Britain is the lion. A lion never has wings. And if you read that Scripture, it not only talks about this lion having wings, but the wings were that of an eagle. The Scripture also tells us that the eagle's wings on the lion were plucked out of the lion. This shows it was not done voluntarily but in a battle. In other words, the war of independence against Great Britain, led by George Washington and the colonies, which had the purpose of Americans gaining freedom from the grip of the lion. To this day, the lion is the symbol of Great Britain, and the coat of arms of the United States is an eagle with two wings spread out, carrying thirteen arrows on one claw, which means the thirteen original colonies had to fight to become independent. On the left claw of the eagle is an olive branch. This means America will always have a powerful military and is always willing to pursue peace whenever possible. The founding fathers who brought about this coat of arms had no idea they were fulfilling the Holy Scriptures, specifically the book of Daniel, verse two through four of chapter seven. Do see how powerful the Bible is and how brutally accurate it is? So, tell me, who are those arrogant people in our midst who, in their ignorance and their inevitable eternal damnation, are still questioning the Bible as the infallible Word of God?

This revelation was given to me by the Spirit of God over a decade ago. It is not possible for a country like the United States to be missing in the Bible given the role it has played for more than two centuries, along with the notable achievements it has had on the world stage. This is especially true when you consider that other empires that had less time on the earth than the United States were mentioned in the Bible. I graduated cum laude from UHG. Now, this is a joke. It stands for University of the Holy Ghost. Enjoy the laughter.

The former American revolutionaries, who were now statesmen, drew up a system of governing that led to the establishment of the three tiers of governing institutions: the executive branch, headed by the president; the legislative branch, which includes the joint Congress; and the judiciary branch, headed by the chief justice. The chief justice was appointed by the president but confirmed by the Senate. The objective was, on one hand, to set up a system of checks and balances to ensure that one branch didn't have excessive power, and on the other hand, the objective was to entrust more power to the people who, through the ballot box, elected the members of these branches, with the exception of the judiciary branch. So how did they go about this?

After the American Revolution, in which George Washington and his brave militia from the thirteen original colonies prevailed over the highly trained and well-respected British Red Coats, they gained their independence on July 4, 1776. The thirteen original colonies then sent representatives to a meeting at what was known as the Philadelphia Convention, and in Independence Hall in Philadelphia, they drew up the Constitution in 1789. It wasn't easy to accomplish this important task. A prior constitution from 1777 had to be replaced with the one that is now in place today. Alexander Hamilton, George Washington, and James Madison—to mention a few—all of whom were nationalists, drew up the Constitution, which led to a more powerful central government while delegating any power the federal government did not have or want to the states. Alexander Hamilton, who was widely regarded as the father of the Constitution, surrounded himself with like-minded men of all persuasions and enterprises to craft the United States Constitution. It is widely believed and verified that many of these men were members of a clergy and devout men of God. So, it came as no surprise that many of the pillars of the Constitution were drawn from inspiration not just from the previous Greek Empire but also from the Bible.

Even today, it is not uncommon to see many federal and state buildings throughout the United States that have quotations taken directly from the Bible, including the chambers of the United States Senate. In fact, the motto of the key electoral battle-state of Ohio is, "With God all things are possible." A 1997 lawsuit challenging its presence went in favor of the state of Ohio. And on our paper currency we have the quote saying, "In God we trust." In the local mall in my suburb in Lewisville, Texas, are the Ten Commandments. Unfortunately, some of our college students, instead of doing research to find out why most of our founding fathers were acknowledging God, are seeking to remove these monuments and scriptural writings that glorify God. They believe that because we have citizens of every country on Earth now living in America, we should not have our Christian heritage splashed on public buildings. They forget that no nation on Earth will settle for this unwise counsel. Neither India or Japan would hide the fact they are a predominantly Hindu nation, nor would Japan hide its Buddhist faith.

The most important component of the Constitution was the various freedoms that were deliberately given to America's citizens. It gave the people who formed the thirteen original colonies a set of freedoms that is unmatched by any nation in the world today, except those nations that have chosen to emulate the American experience. Today, all fifty states that form the United States of America are governed by the Constitution. These cherished freedoms range from freedom of expression to freedom of religion to the right to own your own business to the right to have less intrusion from the federal government in the affairs of individual states. And yes, the one that is so controversial today: the right to bear arms. The American system of government is the embodiment of the devolution of powers. The United

States today is a beacon of hope to the whole world, and it is the shining light on the hill among many other nations.

The U.S., for all practical purposes, has led the world in inventions in agriculture, manufacturing, science, medicine, and technology. Each of the inventions has been transformational and lifechanging. She is the breadbasket of the world and now produces and markets billions of dollars' worth of organic food. She has met every challenge with spectacular success, and the finding of a vaccine for Covid-19 will be carried out with unmatched speed. Her ingenious citizens have built a functioning democracy and have not needed a monarchial system of government. Her products and services have transformed the world for good. Her men and women in the armed forces have defended freedom abroad and saved civilizations from being taken over by ruthless dictators bent on forceful world domination. She has the most formidable and most powerful blue water Navy in the globe. Her nuclearpowered submarines are the quietest ever built, and they carry the most lethal weapons. She has become the envy of many nations. She is feared by her enemies and respected by her friends. In most cases she is the most reliable ally to have. Just ask Israel and Saudi Arabia. Both nations have benefited from immense amounts of military hardware from the United States, which has helped to ensure their continued existence amid wolves in sheep's clothing in the Middle East.

The innovations by the American people have been incredible and have greatly impacted the world. One that has had smashing success is Coca Cola. This soft drink was invented by John Pemberton. Ironically, it was first made from Kola nuts and was used to treat indigestion and help people sober up from hangovers. Today, this drink can be found in every country on Earth. Similarly, the blue denim trousers known as jeans can be found for sale in every nation, and hundreds of different brands have been made. It was two Americas named Jacob Davis and Levi Strauss

12

who brought this material into the world market in 1871. What about Amazon—the world's largest logistics and distribution center of goods, data storage, products, and services through e-commerce? It was America that started e-commerce. This nation went from being a net importer of oil to having the world's largest oil reserve. North Dakota is now one of the most prosperous states per capital because it is now not only the wheat capital of America. Now it is also a state with a lot of oil. If life isn't faring well for you where you live, move to North Dakota if you are not afraid of the cold winters. During my race for governor of Minnesota in 2010, I visited a plant in Brooklyn Park, Minnesota, that had built the first indestructible light bulb, which lasted longer and used less electricity. There are other inventions like the telephone, which was designed by Alexander Bell, and the first light bulb, which was invented by Edison.

Benjamin Franklin, an American, was responsible for pioneering many inventions that transformed the whole world. His notable inventions touched every major area, from musical instruments to medical equipment to electricity to ways to keep streets cleaner. He established America's first liberal college, now known as the University of Pennsylvania. What was so fascinating was that he refused to patent any of them, saying they should be shared freely. He developed the lightning rod to prevent buildings from being struck by lightning, and then he developed bifocal glasses because he had poor eyesight and was tired of switching between two pairs of glasses. Instead of just complaining, Franklin understood the truth that successful people always look for solutions to society's problems, and he acted.

We cannot forget the internet, which was developed by the U.S. military and is now available to the whole world. There are also other ingenious products developed by U.S. citizens, such as the most advanced jet fighters in the world, including planes not visible by radar. The black bird, a supersonic plane that was used during the Cold War to gather intelligence, was, at one time, the fastest jet plane and moved at the speed of sound. Today, the U.S. military and civilian work force both use drones to accomplish their separate agendas. For the U.S. military the drones have been a very effective strategy against terrorism without endangering our fine men and women in uniform, whose heroic work is worthy of adoration and admiration. The major wars American G.I.s have been part of in order to preserve the freedom of other nations is unmatched by any other nation on Earth. Our marines, air force, rangers, special forces, troops, and navy have carried out lifesaving rescue operations on behalf of our country and on behalf of others. America is the land of the free and the home of the brave.

"Freedom and the dignity of the individual have been more available and assured here than in any other place on Earth." -Ronald Reagan

We do not go to war to colonize other nations like Great Britain did, nor do we conquer other nations in order to boast like the feared Roman legion under Julius Caesar did. In most cases we have always had a higher and more noble purpose. We step in to stop dictators like Adolf Hitler from overrunning Europe, or we intervene in order to send a powerful lesson to people like Emperor Hirohito and other would-be future aggressors. Our message to them is that an unprovoked attack on a sovereign nation will not and cannot go unchecked; it must be forcefully repelled and have dire consequences. Anytime you deviate from this principle, it would only serve to embolden the dictator. This is why under President Obama, Russian President Putin annexed part of Ukraine. This took place because Putin saw that the U.S. did next to nothing when he annexed part of Georgia under George W. Bush. Yet America has always maintained a strategic balance between war and peace. I am glad to let you know this great country has had eighteen male and three female recipients of the Nobel Peace Prize. This makes our nation the nation with the highest number of recipients. President Ronald Reagan's policy of peace being strength still rings true to my ears. Almost all of our former presidents—including the current one, I believe—recognized that it is God who has blessed America. The challenge we have is this: Do the young adults of today know this truth. Remember John F. Kennedy, the charismatic, dashing, handsome president who won the hotly contested presidential election in 1960? We learned that his personal life left much to be desired in terms of him being faithful to his wife, Jacqueline Kennedy, who also came from an aristocratic family. Yet Kennedy, a Democrat, knew in his heart that there was a God who rules nations. This is something he said that did not reach the fame his other quotations did, but it just might be remembered in heaven.

"Let us go forth to lead the land we love, asking His blessing and His help, but knowing that here on earth God's work must truly be our own." -John F. Kennedy.

I can assure you that JFK wasn't talking about Buddha or some other god who came and died; he was referring to the immortal, invisible God who dwells in unapproachable light, the one who sent His only begotten Son to die for our sins. Subsequent presidents later acknowledged God in the same way.

On March 30, 1863, Abraham Lincoln declared a national day of prayer and fasting. In the beginning Lincoln was not a leader who openly displayed his faith, unlike some reborn leaders such as George Bush, the 43rd president, and our current president, Donald Trump. And there is absolutely nothing wrong with that. I applaud George Bush for his courage. After all, Jesus Christ says in the Bible, "'Whoever acknowledges me before others, I will also acknowledge before my Father in heaven. But whoever disowns me before others, I will disown before my Father in heaven"

(Mt 10:32-33 NIV). Nevertheless, if you study the biography of Abraham Lincoln, you will realize that the crisis he faced caused him to seek a higher source of nourishment for his weary soul. He needed guidance during unsteady times and wisdom to rule a nation that appeared to be unraveling. This occurred during the most tumultuous period in our nation's history: The American Civil War, in which countless lives were lost to create a more perfect union. It was during this period that Abe Lincoln said, "I have been driven many times upon my knees by the overwhelming conviction that I had no where else to go. My own wisdom and that of all about me seemed insufficient for that day."

There are so many things that have come out of good old U.S.A. There are not enough pages in a book to publish all of it. We are the most resilient people on Earth. Our country has an enduring spirit that has been placed in her by God Himself. The American people are generally observed as easygoing, unpretentious, and, at times, down to earth. Citizens from humble beginnings have become billionaires just for being talented in a particular sport. We are a land with opportunities for all *and* responsibilities for all. As I write, we are in the process of developing a passenger train that would turn a five-hour journey from Dallas, Texas, to Austin, Texas, into a trip less than one hour. Not too long ago, President Trump signed an executive order known as Memorandum 02518. This will help the tech industry gain the upper-hand in Spectrum Technologies, also known as 5G. 5G will make data processing 400 times faster data than it currently is. Its impact would affect our major industries, from airports to hospitals to the auto industry, and it would even affect our household appliances at home. It would create millions and millions of jobs, and revenues could go as high as twelve trillion dollars. 5G will take artificial intelligence to a whole new level.

We are working on a vaccine for Covid-19, moving at a faster rate than any other time in our history when we have developed a vaccine. All of these great transformations have come out of one country, which came to be known as the United States of America on September 9, 1776. I love this country. I have traveled to all of the continents but two. There isn't any nation like America. And what makes this country so great is its people. We are a diverse bunch of folks from all works of life—some rowdy, some quiet, some folksy, some cool, some classy, some hillbilly, some with soul, some Republican, some Democrat, and some Socialist. I think the last two have merged, because you really can't tell the difference these days. Ha ha ha! Just kidding! Please don't get angry; just laugh!

The great news about this Covid-19 dilemma is that the people on the frontlines—our first responders, truck drivers, the daring and bold doctors and nurses, and all those within the supply chain who are part of this army of divine helpers— have been heroic and fearless in their resolve to save as many lives as they can. I can assure you heaven has taken notice. When you hear of nurses from all over the country descending on New York to fight Covid-19, you know this is indeed a very special country with wonderful, truly amazing, great people. Yes, we have our own issues and battles we deal with daily in the U.S., but our country is also made up of extraordinary people doing extraordinary things every single day. We cry together, we laugh together, and we fight together to preserve our freedoms and leave a legacy for future generations. God bless America. Nevertheless, it is critical and important, like never before, that we remain united on the things that bring us together while working to solve the differences that separate us.

The key word here is "united," because as long as we are united and have values similar to what brought our founding fathers together to write our Constitution, we will continue to thrive. If we are divided in the way we are today, and if we begin to turn away from the inalienable

Creator who made us great, our inevitable demise will be written on the wall. This is what I hear the Spirit of the Lord saying. The year 2020 is a year that will be a major game-changer in America's history. This is the time for Christians to strengthen that which remains in them and spend more time on bended knees, fasting and praying for this country, themselves, and family. Take a day off occasionally and eat nothing unless you have to take medications that require you to eat. God will bless you for doing this. Many positive innovations in our country have come out of quiet meditation. Wisdom comes from God, and He imparts it into the heart of the humble, and to his faithful children who ask for it.

What will befall us in 2021 will largely be determined by what we do in 2020. We will either rise up to greater heights than we have ever imagined or fall to a point where we will never be the same again. The alternative to rising to greater heights is that we'll begin to see a steep decline in literally everything that we have enjoyed, including our cherished freedoms. Before Adolf Hitler rose to power, he started by intimidating the government that was in power with his radical followers. He showed a level of intolerance in his views. It was an ominous sign of what eventually unfolded when he came to power. If we're at a point when someone can get fired from a job just because he or she supports the president, this means we are in big, big trouble in America. When a Congress woman is telling people to boycott a successful American entrepreneur's business because he visited the 45th president to discuss how to help our fellow Americans during this pandemic, you know we are in a different time and season in America. Regardless of your political affiliation, you should condemn evil when you see it, or very soon you, too, will soon be a victim of it. When Americans in the service of the current administration in the White House are told they cannot eat in a certain restaurant because of their political affiliations, this is a sign of very

18

terrible things unfolding in the country. I see it this way: No one fears God these days. There is a day of reckoning, and since you and I do not know when we are going to die, we should ask to be forgiven and try to avoid being filled with the spirit of hate and bitterness.

Finally, when the media choose to be silent and deliberately do not comment or criticize these evils taking place in our country, it means we are in trouble. I am not a right-wing conspiracy theorist, and I stay away from websites and talk radio that see conspiracy in everything. Yet I am convinced the one world government that the Bible makes reference to is nearer than we think. Without question, whether you choose to believe it or not, there is indeed a sinister plot to unravel the greatness of this country in other to establish that evil agenda. Since it is written in the Bible, we cannot stop it, but we can try to delay it until the saints are raptured into the third heavens. Yes, we are that close to the beginning of the end times. Who becomes president in 2020 will determine how quickly we will enter the end times and whether our nation will go up or down. This calls for sober reflection and muchneeded prayers. God can use any president of any political party to accomplish His objectives for each nation. He can choose to punish a nation or bless it. So keep your eyes on God through His Son, Jesus Christ, and continuously pray for America.

Satan is jealous and has been for a while, especially about how God has indeed blessed America. For nearly sixty years he has skillfully worked to erode the core values that have pleased God and caused us to be blessed immensely. God has been very lenient on the United States, allowing us more time to repent and, above all, return to our first love. As long as we remained the number one nation on Earth— spreading the gospel through television, mission trips, and other forms of evangelism—God was inclined to look the other way.

However, when we began to celebrate sin (when you are sinning and proud of it) and, even worse, persecute the Christians who opposed the sin, it reached a sore point in God's heart. As if this weren't enough, the division in the country, caused by the media's deception, has really angered the good Lord. God knows, as it is written in His Word, a house divided cannot stand on its own. The spirit of division that has swept this country is unraveling all of our accomplishments and undermining who we are as Americans. The spirit behind it is the spirit of the antichrist and Satan himself. God isn't happy about the division between family members, with parents and children hating each other. This is unacceptable in God's eyes. Remember, when He raised John the Baptist more than 2,000 years ago, it was not only to prepare the way for Christ's arrival on the earth; it was also to reconcile fathers and their children, lest the Lord's anger burn against the nation.

It is written: "'See, I will send the prophet Elijah to you before that great and dreadful day of the Lord comes. He will turn the hearts of the parents to their children, and the hearts of the children to their parents; or else I will come and strike the land with total destruction'" (Mal 4:5-6 NIV).

When I was reborn, I learned that the word "hate" is a very strong word, and God does not want any human being to hate anyone. We should only hate the sins that God hates. Therefore, anyone harboring a spirit of hate toward another human being has a problem with God. Indeed, it is of enormous importance that they resolve this matter before they "kick the bucket" or depart suddenly from this world. Jesus died for the sins of the whole wide world, choosing to forgive our iniquities, and thus you ought to have that same spirit of forgiveness.

Recently, I learned from an interview with ABC from last year that Michelle Obama said in her memoir that she would never forgive Trump and his supporters for the birther movement controversy questioning the citizenship of the 44th

president, her husband. I certainly empathize sincerely with the former first lady. We can only imagine what she went through mentally, physically, and emotionally, including the concern she had for her girls' safety and wellbeing. No one deserves this ugly brand of politics that has unfortunately become all too common in the political discourse in our country. I am sorry this occurred, and it was flat-out wrong. Nevertheless, I write this book as a low-key messenger and servant of the most high God, and I encourage the elegant, fine, brilliant, and polished former first lady to forgive the president and some of his supporters because this is the solemn request of Jesus Christ, who is the Son of God. And I am serious. My prayer is that God, through His Son, will grant Michelle the strength and fortitude to do this so that others will follow in her footsteps and forgive one another, which the Messiah has commanded us to do.

It is written: "For if you forgive other people when they sin against you, your heavenly Father will also forgive you. But if you do not forgive others their sins, your Father will not forgive your sins" (Mt 6:14-15 NIV).

Like her or hate her, many people all over the world still look up to Michelle Obama as a role model to be admired. Therefore, if she starts talking about forgiveness, using what happened to her as a testimony, it could begin to heal our land and transform both our nation and other nations of the world. A person must fear God to forgive. If you do not fear God, you are unlikely to forgive. The world is getting nastier every day, and someone with a meek and gentle heart needs to rise up and remind us all that we were created in God's image and that God is love, so therefore we must walk in love. Regardless of what she chooses to do, may God Himself, through His Son, heal her emotional wounds and the pain Michelle Obama has experienced because of this unfair accusation on her husband. I will be praying for Michelle Obama.

21

I am also be praying that President Trump will one day, before he leaves the earth—and I sincerely wish him a very long life and many happy days— muster the courage and humility to apologize. Jesus Christ is coming very soon, and each one of us must be reconciled with one another and learn to forgive even the most egregious and painful things done to us by others. Let it also be known that some of the most wicked things have been said by millions of Americans against President Donald Trump, and this behavior continues to this day. The hatred they have for him is unacceptable in the eyes of God. Hatred, unforgiveness, and bitterness are very poisonous to the human soul and body. Even worse, you disqualify yourself from entering the Kingdom of heaven when you die or leave this world, even if you gave billions of dollars to help the poor globally. It is written: "Whoever claims to love God yet hates a brother or sister is a liar. For whoever does not love their brother and sister, whom they have seen, cannot love God, whom they have not seen. And he has given us this command: Anyone who loves God must also love their brother and sister" (1 Jn 4:20-21 NIV).

Now, let me be crystal clear. We have all sinned and come short of God's glory. There isn't one perfect person on earth. Each one of us is in need of repentance. There is always something we need to work on. God is love, and we are created in His image, and thus we must carry that love wherever we go. Let's face it: We are all in need of God's mercy and grace, period. That said, don't advertise your sins to other nations or choose to celebrate your sins, lest you provoke the anger of your Father.

America has been the embodiment and personification of absolute greatness. Everything we put our minds to always ends up being the best of the best. We know how to have a good time. People from nations all over the world now call America their home. They all came to live a better life. People from India, Nigeria, Afghanistan, England, Italy,

22

Brazil, Ireland, Malta, Argentina, Kazakhstan, and many other places have all come to dwell in this richly blessed land of ours. Now, in no part of the Constitution is it written that we should subscribe to their ways of life or worship their gods in order to remain great. This would be insane, as they came here because of who we are. Yes, we can learn different things from other nations that will further enrich our lives. But we can do it without erasing our own culture heritage, and we should never bring a curse upon our land by subscribing to things in those nations that God hates. Now, let those who have ears hear what the Spirit of the Lord is saying.

Let Us Pray

My God and my King. Eternal Rock of Ages. El Olam, the everlasting God, I come before you this day in the name of Jesus Christ, your only begotten Son, also known as Yeshua in Hebrew. He is the name above all other names in heaven and on earth. I humbly ask for Your forgiveness for any acts of indiscretion; iniquity; guilt; lawlessness; disobedience; rebellion, such as witchcraft; deliberate sinning; unconscious sinning; bitterness; and unforgiveness toward others. I ask this on behalf of the American people as well. Do not judge us in Your anger; instead, have mercy on us as a nation because it was Christ who died and rose from the dead, and He now sits at Your right side, interceding for us. Thank you for making us the longest serving democracy on Earth as well as one of the most prosperous nations since the beginning of time. We do

not have enough words to express our profound sense of gratitude and appreciation. All we can say is this: You have been a good Father and an awesome God to America. Now, sovereign Lord, even in the midst of the great darkness that shall cover the earth before your Son returns, as has been written in the Bible, let Your perfect will be done on Earth,

23

as it is written of America in heaven. Even if judgment is inevitable for America, temper Your fierce anger with mercy because it is written about You, Lord, and You cannot deny that Your mercy endures forever. So have mercy on America. Yes, Lord, let Your light shine forth ever so brightly over my life and America so that other nations may see Your good works again and then glorify Your name. In Your Son's name we pray. Amen and amen.

Chapter 2

RACISM IS A SPIRIT, AND IT COMES FROM SATAN

Racism is a spirit that comes from the pit of hell, and it originates from Satan. The spirit itself is invisible to the naked eye, but its diabolical menace on its victims is real and very visible. Sometimes it is subtle, such as in the workplace, and at times it is very visible, like police brutality. It is difficult for anyone who hasn't experienced it to fully understand what victims of racism go through. Today, racism is based primarily on stereotypes and false assumptions. We allow false narratives to occupy and rent space in our minds without realizing we are sinning against the Almighty God, El Shaddai. For example, we say black people are lazy and always come late to work. All white folks are just plain racist, or America is a racist country. Asians hate blacks, and we know it. The list of these incorrect and false assumptions goes on and on. Our language has sometimes fueled and fed this real spirit of racism. Being racist means you are questioning God's wisdom, because He created all beings in His likeness and image. He then chose to make different skin colors. If you still are unable to grasp this truth, you might want to watch some previous episodes of W Kamau Bell, who was the host of the CNN show *United Shades of America*.

Since God is sovereign and knows the end from the beginning and the beginning from the end, He knew slavery

25

would come upon the earth and that nations like America would unfortunately be part of it. God hates the oppression of one man by another man or one nation by another nation. Let us not forget that Satan is the god of this world and of this age. Until his final elimination from the earth takes place, as written in the book of Revelation in the Bible, he rules through deception and the power we humans give him through our sins against God. Slavery was very much part of American history, as our ancestors acquired slaves from Africa. Shame on those Africans who sold their sons and daughters to slavery; they cannot be exempt from the problem. Many of these American slave owners went to church and called themselves Christians. Yet, based on what I have read in the Bible, the way they treated their slaves was clearly outside the will of God. They saw fellow human beings of a different skin color as a commodity to be traded in the market square. They did not realize they were partaking in a trade in the "market square of Satan." They traded the souls of men. The United States government and its people have since been at work trying to rectify this dark side of our history, yet what is needed the most is for Americans to have a change of heart toward one another. This work must be led by the church, and it will indeed take the power of God to end systemic racism in the fabric of our society. Yes, it will also take the fear of God to demolish this stronghold in the hearts of millions of Americans. Racism is evil in the eyes of God. Having said this, God is not unaware of the strides we have made as a nation to rectify the problem and ameliorate race relations. From non-governmental organizations to the highest level of our government, we have made tremendous progress, but much more needs to be done. This may sound like nonsense and empty philosophy in light of the recent demonstration following the murder of George Floyd in Minneapolis, Minnesota.

Yet I am emphatic in saying America has indeed come a long way, and today we can boast of many things that we have done right to improve race relations and create a more perfect union. We have placed prominent black leaders in all spears of our economy. Many black entrepreneurs have risen to the highest corporate ladder in America, heading major fortune 500 companies. The dream of the late Martin Luther King has been fulfilled. Millions of African Americans and Caucasians work together, laugh together, attend sports games together, and go to church together, even though the church is still one of the most segregated places in America. Yet progress has been made on all fronts and in every job sector. Many barriers have been broken, and glass ceilings have been shattered. Stereotypes, as I mentioned earlier, are the last lingering block that needs to be eliminated from each of our hearts, and we will get to where we no longer see each other first through the prism of color. Instead, we will see each other for our character.

It was America that chose to shatter the white glass ceiling by voting a black man in as president. We elected an American from African descent as president of the United States in 2008, then reelected him 2012. Rev. Jesse Jackson's unsuccessful bid in 1988 showed America that this was possible, as he was the runner up to the late Michael Dukakis in the democratic primary race in 1988. He, more than anyone, paved the way for President Barack Obama. The majority of the votes for our former president were cast by white folks. So how can one genuinely say that all white folks are racist? Many of these same Caucasian voters then turned around and voted for Trump in 2016, so how can you say Trump won because white racists voted for him?

What about the 1.6 million blacks who voted for him, too? Were they also racists? Bitterness in politics is also stirring the evil cauldron of racism, and this is unfortunate because it affects the unity of our country. The mainstream media could help if only they were willing to abandon their political biases, which are really dividing our nation and hurting our country.

27

While America has made great strides, it is no secret that a lot more still needs to be done in order to improve race relationships, lest the wrath of God burn against this great nation. God has a deep, avid hatred for racism. God's anger burns even more when a black or ethnic people are racist toward Caucasians, because, out of everyone, they should know better.

Reverse racism is also very much in our midst, and it is not justified either. It is based in the spirit of bitterness. I say this because I know many black people who think it is justifiable when it is not. You cannot blame all the problems in the African American community on racism. We have a moral obligation to fess up and take ownership for our shortcomings, especially in terms of our moral rectitude and the choices we make in life, especially in the last sixty years. I'm referring to some of the decisions made by many in the black community that go against the traditional family unit and the values that have kept our country steady. You cannot blame racism for out-of-wedlock pregnancies that sometimes lead to poverty and subsidized living. You cannot fault the U.S. government when irresponsible men recklessly impregnate women with no intention of raising the child that is born. Let's face it: There is a huge incarceration rate in the black community, and it's not *just* because of an unjust justice system. It is also because of people not having the right upbringings due to the high rate of absentee fatherly figures. Life has consequences based on the choices we make and the directions we go in life. As the saying goes, where you are in life today is based on the choices you made along the journey of life. Then there are the decisions made by some young women who are unfortunately not aware that their bodies do not belong to them but to the God Almighty. Due to poor self-esteem, lack of appropriate role models, and other external factors, they end up having children from so many different partners because they are lonely. Yes, we are all imperfect human beings, and we all have our shortcomings. Yet every day we have an opportunity to make right choices and wrong choices. We sure do like to take credit for the right choices, don't we? Yet it is so easy to shift the blame for the consequences of our mistakes and poor choices in life on others and on society in general. I know myself; if I had not had a strong father and a strict mother, I would have been in trouble. The few years I spent with my parents set me on a path to achieving something great. I am fully aware there are many single parents who have raised extraordinary kids, but it isn't easy, and they will be the first to tell you that.

My mother died when I was seven years old, and I lost my father at the age of 25. At the beginning of my early childhood, we did not have much. My parents had six kids. I remember only wearing shoes when I was going to school, then taking them off when I came back home from school. In fact, while playing with my brothers and sisters, I sustained a small cut on my left pinky toe when I hit it on a small stone on the ground. I had no shoes on. Then a little African bug, along with its bacteria, entered the injured toe through the open wound. I was in trouble. My grandmother treated it by using a sterilized razor blade and some ointment. She cut the skin of the toe and removed the bug. It was a painful experience and an unforgettable one.

I remember going to a local shoemaker with my mother to get sandals for my twin brother and me, then buying imported ones from the department store. This was in the late sixties and early seventies in Africa, so they would have been more expensive. My mother passed away due to a brief illness, way too early for any child to lose a mother. I can still remember her very well. The few short years we spent together were enough to teach me about right and wrong. I remember misbehaving and getting spanked. I also remember that she was a beautiful woman and a very loving mother. She was a sixth-grade elementary school teacher in the same elementary school my brothers, sisters, and I attended. We were trained from childhood not to do anything to embarrass her or our name. I can still remember the funeral. It was the first casket I had seen in my life. As we walked into the church, I saw a casket close to the altar at the Catholic church in the University of Ibadan. My late father asked all of us, "Do you know who is in this casket?" We all said no. "It is your mother. She is dead," he told us. And then we took our seats in the front row. I did not cry. I was just sad. It was too much for a kid to absorb. On my 37th birthday, I wept so much because my mother had died at the age of thirty-six and I had been able to get past that age. That was the first time I cried over the death of my mother — thirty years after her death. I was so miserable, and I could not be comforted. I stopped crying when I began to thank God for allowing me to live past my mother's age. I was grateful. Too many single moms take their anger with the deadbeat father of their child and pour it out on the child. This is wrong and sometimes makes children think no one cares for them and that they were born to emulate the flaws of their fathers. Unfortunately, spiritually, there is a truth to this. There are certain sins we commit that end up transferring to our children and subsequent generations.

In the early 60s the late Senator Patrick Monyihan of New York wrote a piece about the crisis that was engulfing the black community, saying a bleak picture awaited their future if it wasn't halted. He was writing about the decision that some members of our community had made to abandon the traditional family role. He also discussed the consequences this posed, such as family instability and the deterioration of the wellbeing of the black community, and how this could perpetuate a cycle of poverty and deprivation. The honorable senator was widely criticized and condemned by the main press, but with time those who had earlier criticized him began to see the foresight of his report after looking at how many families with single parents had indeed struggled to keep their children from entering into the prison system. Yes, there are always exceptions and heroic stories of single mothers, regardless of race, raising their children to become responsible adults. Prior to the Civil Rights movement, the black community had the lowest divorce rate, and the sin of bringing children into the world out of wedlock was rare. Having said this, as a black man, I have some empathy for the black community. How can you blame them when black people often encounter Caucasians who discriminate against them because of the color of their skin?

I have read articles in various magazines about rich Hollywood actors who, because they were black, were stopped by the police for driving a nice vehicle that the Caucasian policemen did not believe they owned or deserved to be driving. Now this is very sad and unfortunate. In the eyes of God, this is wrong and racist. Cops who do this don't realize they are being watched from heaven. In spite of this lingering problem in our society, there are ways people of color can avoid becoming victims and having their lives cut short by aggressive police officers on the beat. It does not work all the time, but it can help. Try, as much as possible, to conduct yourself in a way that breaks down the stereotype cops generally have about black people when they stop them. For example, I do admit that because of my upbringing, I learned how to be polite, truthful, and proper, and I learned to conduct myself in a dignified way that conveys respect to authorities. So it goes without saying that, with the exception of one occasion, each time I was stopped by cops in any city in America while driving, it was because I was speeding and not because I was black. This is the honest truth.

I have been lucky enough to visit forty-four states in America. This great country has so much to offer to tourists who come from all over the world to visit. This may be very hard for my African American brothers and sisters to believe, yet it is 100% accurate that police officers pulled me over not because I was black but because I was not driving withing the speed limit. I am not talking about five miles above the speed limit; they never pulled me over for that. The second truth may even be harder to swallow, and it is indeed an amazing real-life experience: ninety percent of the time, the cops let me go without issuing me a ticket. They occasionally gave me a warning ticket. That changed when I came to Texas; I have still gotten some free passes, but not as many as when I spent twenty-seven years in Minnesota. The cops loved me there. Indeed, I had mastered the ability to disarm their concern about their safety when they saw a black man in the car. I would quickly read the name on the uniform, then greet the officer politely by saying something like, "Hello, Officer Tim!" My Caucasian friends in Minnesota can testify to this truth, as some of them were in the car with me. I will make bets with them and say, "I am never going to get a ticket. You watch." And that is exactly what would happen. I was fully aware of trigger-happy cops, and I was determined not to be a victim. I believe deep in my heart that God's grace on my life protected me from this. I often prayed, and I would first apologize to God for speeding. I have a heavy right foot, and I am working on driving within the speed limit because my wife doesn't really care much for all that fast driving and foolishness. Nevertheless, for me it is a living testimony of the goodness of the Lord in the land of the free and the home of the brave.

All of us, regardless of the color of our skin, must do what we can to avoid being racist. We must fear God. We must avoid grieving the Holy Spirit. Each one of us need to become part of the solution to this human race problem that began 400 years ago in our country. The time has come for all of us to deal with this problem head on, and the church must take a lead role in eliminating this evil in our country and ending all forms of discrimination based on race. Our lives are being recorded in heaven, and the day of judgment draws near.

Racism is ugly, it is unfair, it is wicked, it is abusive, it is condescending, and it can be brutal and even lead to outright murder. It is based on a false sense of pride—thinking you are better than others because of your skin color. Now, some would argue that the last statement may have a small element of truth within it when it comes to certain sports. Yes, this is true that in some sports black folks perform better than people of other races. Now this doesn't mean you cannot find Caucasians who can perform just as good in the same sports. The reverse is also true. Can I keep it real here? For example, most blacks and people of color, to a large extent, do not excel in skiing and water sports, unlike their Caucasian counterparts. This doesn't mean you can't find blacks who can't play basketball but like to swim and ski. I'm one of those people!

I'm sure you have heard of *White Men Can't Jump*, the movie starring Wesley Snipes. Well, I am the black man who can't jump. Therefore, assuming all black folks know how to play basketball is wrong. You get the point. We need to stop stereotyping and start treating people based on who they are rather than making assumptions based on the color of their skin. What is the difference between racism and discrimination? Racism is disliking someone outright because they do not look like you. Discrimination is showing preferential treatment or disqualifying someone because of the color of their skin. When Asians and Caucasians are denied by Ivy Leagues because these institutions want to meet their quota of minorities, primarily black and Hispanic students, they are being discriminated against. This is the truth, and let's not play games here. On the other hand, I am not against these campuses trying to create a diverse student population.

Satan, also known as Lucifer, was an angelic being and was head of the angels in heaven before he fell.

33

This was millions of years ago. The first three verses of chapter one of Genesis take place more than seven thousand years ago, but this is another story for another day.

It is written: "And he made from one every nation of men to live on all the face of the earth, having determined allotted periods and the boundaries of their habitation..." (Acts 17:26 RSV).

Nevertheless, when Satan learned that God was going to create you and me in God's image, he was jealous and has been jealous since then. He could not wait to deceive Adam and Eve. He is the father of racism, and anyone who dies a racist is going to hell. No ifs, ands, or buts. The root of racism is hatred for another person who does not look like you but was created by God. Now, in America we have run into a major problem, and that is, rather than dealing with the heart of the matter, we blame almost every dispute involving blacks and other races on racism or discrimination. This is ridiculous, and this does not bode well for our society. Further, it fractionalizes us as a country and unfairly stigmatizes others. It is wrong to see everything under the prism of racism, and unfortunately, many African Americans have gravitated toward that deception. They need to reconsider their thought process. The Bible says, "For as he thinketh in his heart, so is he..." (Prv 23:7 KJV). In other words, if you become so obsessed with attributing every challenge in your life to racism, you will never make any progress in life.

Now, let me be crystal clear: We all have our prejudices and biases. No one is immune. God is working in all of us, helping us see our fellow brethren the way God sees them. It is God who made us all. Light has seven different colors, and when you are a racist, even if it is hidden, you are butting heads with God and literally telling him, "How dare you create another color for a human being." You see the arrogance, stupidity, and pride in such an individual. It is only when you are reborn that you can be proud of

34

your skin color and, at the same time, appreciate someone who is different from you. Today, we have Caucasians who actually deny their skin color or feel guilty that they were born white. They think it is progressive, but it is quite frankly foolish and deceptive. They have also become an impediment to ending the stigma of racism in America in a dignified way.

As I pointed out earlier on, racism comes into a person as a spirit. It doesn't matter whether it was fostered from childhood or learned from becoming part of a gang. It can also come from a person who isn't happy with himself and is therefore looking to focus on another person's shortcomings in order to justify his own failed and miserable life. You can educate society about not being racist, but it is a change of heart that removes the spirit from a person who is racist. Jesus is in the heart business, and Jesus is the only known person who, with God, created the human heart. You know you cannot say you love God and be a racist. I am not saying it did not happen hundreds of years ago. Yes, many slave owners went to church, but they were deceived by Satan. Any form of slavery is dehumanizing. Today, we have sex slaves in many countries in Asia, Africa, and Eastern Europe. Right here at home, we have prostitution rings that specialize in young boys, girls, and runaway teenagers. This, too, is an outrage and is wrong.

Recently, our nation has unfortunately been rocked by a series of events involving race, in which a black man has been unfairly targeted and killed by cops who were sworn to protect the citizens of their district. I believe this is a precursor to the end times, and it's also a wakeup call to America, telling us to turn to God, lest Satan will sift us like wheat. These actions were unjustified, and one of them was nerve-wrenching and horrible to observe. Yes, the killing of George Floyd by a Minneapolis police officer while his colleagues watched was inhuman at best and satanic at

35

worst. The violence that followed after by protesters was also part of Satan's ploy to embarrass America.

Why do I believe this was the work of Satan? Number one: The police officer named Derek Chauvin, whose knee was pinned on top of George Floyd's neck, knew he was being filmed and videoed, and he did not seem to care. Number two: George Floyd was under control and handcuffed, no longer resisting arrest, and all that needed to be done, if he had done anything wrong, was to put him into the police car. Number three: The other cops, along with others who stood guard so no one could stop the murder, had been infiltrated by Satan. I believe the one cop standing guard was an Asian American. Satan did this to bring division among blacks and Asian Americans. Number four: It cast the United States in a dark light around the world, fueling the false narrative that our leaders, right up to the president, were responsible for this. Yet President Trump does not have oversight or control over individual states' local police forces, nor do any of the previous presidents. Number five: It was designed by Satan to impact the upcoming presidential elections negatively and to introduce race in the ballot box. How unfortunate.

Yet many of you would be stunned if I told you I was the least surprised about what transpired on the streets of North Minneapolis, which has provoked anger throughout the world. If you are a Christian with a deep personal relationship with God, God shares things with you before they take place on the earth. Therefore, less than a month before the ill-fated incident involving George Floyd, I received an important phone call from a close confidant who was also an intercessor and a prayer warrior. She is a lady that decrees and declares and knows her position in the heavenly realm. We often pray together. We both have had our share of demonic harassment and attacks because of our relationship with El Gibor, the all-powerful God. She called to inform me to pray for America and the president because there was a series of events about to unfold in the nation that would create unnecessary disturbance and further divide our nation. She went on to say that it was spiritual. This meant that the culprit behind it, even though there would be humans involved, would be Satan. She then mentioned that I needed to include prayers about racism and the discrimination of women. She said to pray about issues pertaining to the LBGTQ movement and an assassination attempt on President Trump.

Now, I had been praying about the latter for a while, as I did for President Obama when he was president, but the others were news to me. I regret that I did not devote as much steadfast prayer and fasting to these serious issues as they deserved, even though I still prayed for peace and calm. So, I am sorry to say that there is indeed more drama coming up before the 2020 election, but it can be avoided if we remain fervent in prayer. The recent ruling by the Supreme Court that banned discrimination against the LGBTQ helped us avoid what could have been another turbulent time in our country. So prayer opens your heart to the heavenly realm, and you can see things before they even manifest physically. I bet the director of the NSA would like to have that gift, wouldn't he?

Prayer moves mountains. Prayer is a spiritual battle axe. Prayer subdues physical challenges. Prayer levels mounting crises. Prayer is the answer to generational problems. Prayer builds your faith. Prayer brings Christ into your crises. Prayer brings about the necessary wisdom to tackle and resolve intractable problems. Prayer and fasting block the work of Satan on Earth. Prayer can bring about the changes we all desire in terms of improved race relations. And finally, prayer is the ultimate and awesome power that moves the mighty hand of God. The Bible tells us to pray in and out of season. All of us need to examine ourselves and remove any stereotypes we have about people based on their race or gender. There is a God in heaven who frowns on judgmental people.

It is written: "'Do not judge, or you too will be judged. For in the same way you judge others, you will be judged, and with the measure you use, it will be measured to you" (Mt 7:1-2 NIV).

When you are a racist, you are passing judgment on someone because God made them different from you. You are also criticizing God's creation, which is a terrible thing to do. Most racists have no fear of God. How do I know this? Because it is written in the Bible that the fear of God is the beginning of wisdom. If you have wisdom, you know better than to participate in or tactically support a racist agenda from any person, department, workplace, academic institution, or police department. We can see the spirit of Satan at work in America today, especially when it comes to disguised racism based on a false stereotype. For example, when George Floyd was killed by the irresponsible Officer Chauvin, many people took to the streets to vent their anger. In the beginning the majority of them were African Americans, but with time other races and fringe groups took advantage of the situation and joined the African Americans, and mass chaos ensued.

To my surprise the current mayor of Minneapolis, along with the police chief and their counterparts in Seattle, made a mistake in their decision not to intervene at the beginning of the outbreak of violence in North Minneapolis and Seattle. This also led to a socalled temporary takeover of a swarth of territory by lawless mobs in Seattle called "Chop." The goal was to allow the rioters to let out some steam. This was indirect racism in its ugliest form, notwithstanding the fact that the police chief in Seattle is black and the rioters were comprised of all races, not just African Americans. The law enforcement departments in both liberal cities abandoned their sworn fidelity to keep the community safe. In so doing, these leaders created the impression that they do not believe in their hearts that African Americans can peacefully protest. Yet we have shown in the past, and even in these perilous times, that we can peacefully protest. For almost two months now, some parts of the city of Portland have not seen a day of peace, and rioting, looting, and burning of buildings have continued following the death of George Floyd. The mainstream media have embarked on the greatest censorship in American history by hiding it from the American people and downplaying the violence while anarchy reigns in cities, mostly because these cities are run by mayors from the democratic party. The city officials in the above-mentioned cities, in their earlier inaction, prevented the police from doing their job, which is to protect the innocent people of North Minneapolis, Seattle, and Portland. They failed to prevent the destruction of businesses, some owned by African Americans. By being passive, they were saying, "Let the black folks release their anger and vent for a while because of the grotesque way in which George Floyd died." In their unwillingness to get the situation under control quickly at the beginning of the rioting, they were implying we blacks cannot be cool, calm, and collected. In other words, we are not capable of behaving like the late Martin Luther King or leading a peaceful protest similar to the one led by Rev. Jesse Jackson in the past. They were saying, in their inaction, that President Barack Obama, who learned to be calm in the eye of the storm, is an exception and that most blacks are "just violent." They were sending a message that African Americans cannot express their grievances without destroying innocent lives and property. They were giving tactical approval to the "angry black man syndrome," and this is stereotype based on racism. Let's not play games here. Let's call a spade a spade and a rose a rose, especially when it smells like a rose.

In a nutshell, these authorities fuel the incorrect stereotype that we black people do not know how to vent or protest any grave injustice done to us without resorting to violence and the destruction of other people's property. The mainstream media's actions, with the exception of a

39

few, also left much to be desired. Unfortunately, a lot of the media were more interested in seeing this anarchy spread to other parts of the country and allowing things to get chaotic because they were convinced it would negatively impact President Trump. What is at stake is the negative impact this is having on the world.

Even Iran, which has an oppressive regime, was condemning us not only for the Floyd death but also for the aftermath. Two wrongs do not make a right. All of us, regardless of our political differences, must speak with one voice when we see events in our country that are just not right.

My heart goes out to the police officers who died randomly and needlessly by the hands of angry people following Floyd's death. These police officers have families, too, and they had no idea that their last day on Earth would come so soon. The mainstream media showed very little coverage of their deaths, mostly because it was "open season" on police officers in America. One of the most frightening things unfolding in America is how some of our media outlets only report what they want you to hear. Their goal is no longer to report unbiased news; they want to intentionally push their narrative on you, alter your mindset, and influence you to vote a certain way. But the American people are beginning to see through this wicked deception.

The truth is that millions of blacks did not support the destruction of other people's businesses or the shooting of innocent police officers. African Americans, and millions of other Americans, do not support the two attorneys in New York who threw a Molotov cocktail into a police vehicle. Satan exploited this situation to further divide our country, and he hasn't changed, for this is his character. He is a deceiver, and he looks for human proxies, even in the government, to deceive into doing his bidding.

40

Removing the statues of historical figures who were somehow associated with segregation is clearly not the answer to solving the problem of racism in America. It will not stop the police from using excessive force against minorities. The recent shooting of Jacob Blake—he was shot seven times in the back by a police officer while his children watched—in Kenosha, Wisconsin, underscores my point. During the first press conference following the senseless shooting, Jacob's mother's pastor, Juliana Jackson, alluded to the fact that it was a symptom of a spiritual problem in America. Satan is a wicked spirit, and he is entering into people's hearts, like the police officer's, to release murder and mayhem, and God is allowing it because of the sins of this nation. We need to pray and repent. These symbolic changes further divide our nation and do little to save the lives of black men who encounter racist cops and become victims of police brutality. Even worse, the removal of statues of historical figures who fought against slavery is quite frankly foolish and irresponsible. The people who did this do not care about minority rights, nor do they genuinely desire to save black lives. They are anarchists with an evil agenda that is incongruous to the values of mainstream America. Therefore, the defacing of Mathias Baldwin in Philadelphia was wrong because he was a bold abolitionist. The spirit behind meaningless chaos and violence is also Satan. My wife, Juanita Idusogie, put something on Facebook about some of the non-peaceful demonstrations. She said, "We can remove flags and statues all day, but until we figure out how to remove the hate in people's hearts, nothing will change". The good news is that there were just as many, if not more, peaceful protests across the country calling for police reform, and this was indeed the American spirit at its best because people from all races and ethnic groups joined the protest. The power behind racism is Satan, and he is an invisible spirit, thus you cannot see him physically.

41

When Cain killed Abel, as recorded in the book of Genesis, it was the first recorded murder in human history, and it was the beginning of Adam and Eve's consequences for disobeying God. When a nation or person falls under the spirit of disobedience, it gives Satan the power to do certain things to that person or the nation that he otherwise cannot do. The true biblical story goes like this: Cain and Abel were the offspring of Adam and Eve. They each had an opportunity to present a thanksgiving offering to God. Abel, being the wise one and a generous giver, gave his best sheep as a sacrifice to God. Cain was not in the business of animal husbandry. (Let me guess...he was a vegetarian. I am just kidding!) He was a skilled farmer who cultivated and harvested a wide variety of vegetables. I believe they were organic or naturally grown, as there were no pesticides or bugs to prey on the crops when they were ripe for harvest. He prepared an offering of vegetables that left much to be desired. I don't know what it constituted, but God did not look favorably on Cain's offering, unlike He did with his brother Abel. I don't believe it was because God is a meat eater. Cain was stingy and didn't revere God like Abel did. Now, before he slew his brother, they probably got along very well. God called Cain after rejecting his offering, and warned him that sin was going to overtake his heart but that he could overcome it. In other words, Satan had already entered into Cain and had introduced a jealous spirit that grew to be a full-blown murderous spirit. Since God does not take away our free choice, Cain ended up killing his brother in a murderous rage.

As if this weren't enough, when God asked Cain where his brother was, he replied, "Am I my brother's keeper?" What?! He was talking to the most powerful God in the universe. God then told Cain that his brethren's blood was crying on the ground for vengeance. Anytime you take an innocent life, whether it was gang violence or random murder or premeditated murder, the blood on the ground and in the abortion clinics cries out for vengeance. There comes a time when this gets too much and God has to intervene. As you can see, in this true biblical story, the spirit of Satan entered Cain, and he did what a normal person would not do and eventually killed his only brother. This is why the Bible says Satan was a murderer from the beginning. Now, to most biblical scholars, Satan entered Cain for a different reason. He believed Jesus Christ was going to come out of the genealogy of Abel, and he sought to abort that agenda, but he was wrong. Jesus Christ came onto the earth from the genealogy of Seth, the third son of Adam.

When I watched the video of the police officer Derek Chauvin literally murdering George Floyd by placing his knee on his neck, I knew he wasn't going to stop until he had killed George. The spirit of Satan had taken over his dark heart. That same spirit had engulfed the heart of his fellow cops, who stood to protect Officer Derek from an angry gathering crowd rather than restraining him. It would be terribly wrong in the eyes of God not to prosecute those officers, too. Their refusal to restrain their colleague shows they were accomplices to murder. In light of this fact, what do we do to assure a weary nation that this won't happen again?

Physically, we can prosecute Officer Chauvin and his accomplices to the full extent of the law, making an example of all of them. I am not sure it would have an impact on the isolated cases of police brutality or that it would clean up the bad eggs in the police force nationwide. We can protest against the president, who has absolutely no control of the local police force in each state. I say this because one of the political parties is using this terrible saga to convince voters to vote against the president because of his strong words against the rioters who engaged in mass violence and the destruction of property. Quite frankly, it is the city mayors, the chiefs of police, the superintendents of the cities, and the elected judges, most of whom are Democrats, who should

43

be replaced. They were in charge when all of this took place. If the head of the fish is rotten, the whole fish is rotten.

The president is limited in what he can do. He can get more federal oversight for our nation's cops by using the office of the Attorney General. Secondly, he can ask the FBI to investigate systemic racism in the Minneapolis Police Force. Otherwise, let it be known, these police officers are under local authority, and the cities in which they function are under the states to which they belong. Not everyone in the whole world is aware of how our police system is set up in America. Therefore, out of a lack of knowledge, they blame Trump. This is because most places around the world have a federal police system, and all police report to a Federal Inspector General of Police, and the police leaders report to the head of state in most nations. But this is not the case in America. We believe in devolution of government.

Nevertheless, there needs to be a balance. We need to express our strong support for the police while, in the same breath, warning them to avoid anything that would stain or tarnish their reputations and create distrust in the eyes of the public. Even when God was examining the seven churches in the book of Revelation, with the exception of the church of Philadelphia, he talked about something good they were doing and something that was bad or needed to change. Supporting the police without publicly scolding them when they abuse the uniform and code of conduct will accomplish nothing and will not help foster confidence in the police. All lives matter regardless of whether it is a police officer's life or a victim of police brutality. This is not a race or police issue alone, even though the most aggrieved here are people of color. Black lives matter, especially because they have been victims of police brutality for a long time. Nothing has been done in the past to address this injustice, until President Trump, who used executive orders to introduce major police reform, which previous presidents ignored.

44

In general, it is fair to say that most police officers mean well and take their duties seriously. However, if you do not have a relationship with God through His Son, Jesus, and if you do not believe in a higher authority apart from yourself, you become a law unto yourself. You are then more vulnerable to being taken over by Satan and that spirit of racism when you least expect it.

It is written: "Be alert and of sober mind. Your enemy the devil prowls around like a roaring lion looking for someone to devour" (1 Pt 5:8 NIV).

This is possible, especially when you are a cop patrolling the streets and something comes up that requires your involvement. Emotions often run high in these situations. Police officers' heart rates and adrenaline go up, as their jobs are risky. The next thing you know, the unexpected happens, and a life is needlessly lost. The aftermath is someone's career being permanently ruined. Too many police officers' lives have been lost needlessly in the line of duty in America. And yes, too many black lives have also been lost because of trigger-happy police officers. This is true regardless of whether the police get acquitted in court. God is the judge of all, and He is not a Republican or a Democrat. He is judge of all, and the Bible tells us that everyone, without exception, will have to give an account of what they have done with their bodies, whether good or bad. So take heed, America.

Remember, one thing about Satan is that as soon as he has completed his agenda, he leaves you. Then you are left to deal with the consequences of your actions. In the aftermath you keep asking yourself what got into you and made you do this evil thing. Think about the lady in the park in New York who called the cops on an African American photographer. He was just minding his own business and taking photographs of nature. When she was asked why she exhibited such racist behavior, she said she did not know. You see, it is an invisible spirit, and once it enters you, it can ruin your life. So, how does this spirit of racism enter certain

45

people and not others? You first must have an open door. Satan is the master of looking through your bloodline to see if your forefathers and mothers were racists. Therefore, the door of prejudice might be open in you. Today, millions of Americans are fascinated and curious about their ancestry, and have looked into their DNA to find out where they were originally from. The reborn Christians find out through deliverance ministry what iniquity did to our forefathers and what it is now doing in our lives today. I am sharing this secret with everyone reading this book because Satan knows our histories. If the FBI can build a profile of a person, the ruler of the kingdom of darkness can do even more. If you struggle with prejudice and think you are better than others because of your ethnic background or color, you will become a wide-open door for the devil. Today, Officer Chauvin is on suicide watch because of his murderous, unprovoked actions. His wife filed for divorce immediately. The racism that was in him for so long finally reached its maturity, and it ended with the death of a man. The Bible tells us that when sin reaches its maturity, it leads to death. Officer Chauvin's job died that day, and his life will now be miserable unless he gives his life to Jesus Christ and Christ heals him with His balm of Gilead. His marriage and his lifelong aspirations died that day as well. It doesn't matter that George Floyd was being pursued for using counterfeit money and that he had a prior criminal record, including years of previous incarceration. All of that got lost in the aftermath of his death. Therefore, I call racism a sin. It is an oppressive, divisive, deceptive tool of the devil.

Let Us Pray

Jehovah Rapha—the Lord, my healer—You said in Your Word, "If a house is divided against itself, that house cannot stand" (Mk 3:25 NIV). In other words, it would eventually crumble from within, without a single shot fired

46

by an outside enemy. For many years you have blessed America beyond measure, and we grew to become the most powerful nation on Earth. Economically and politically, we became the nation to look up to. Today, we see cracks in our democracy, and we are divided like never before. Anger, hatred, sexual exploitation of young children, bitterness, anarchy, and racism abound in the land, and our politicians are unable to mend fences among the people. Independent media is all but lost in our country. They have all chosen sides rather than standing as independent voices for the people. It is obvious that we have sinned against You. Each person has turned to his own ways, ignorant of Your laws and precepts. I come boldly to the throne of grace to obtain mercy and grace from You. We need Your help. Please forgive our sins—all of our sins— Heavenly Father. Forgive us for the almost sixty-two million abortions we have performed in America. Indeed, forgive us for the 900 daily abortions of black unborn babies. There have been eighteen million of these abortions since Roe v. Wade. We know that nothing can justify this shedding of blood, and we do not want to face the consequences for this dreadful sin in the black community and in America at large. We'll return to You so You can mend our hearts and reconcile us with each other. We ask for Your help in the name above all other names, and that is the name of Jesus. Amen.

Chapter 3

ALL HAVE SINNED. THERE IS NO PERFECT PERSON ON THE EARTH

It is written: "For all have sinned, and come short of the glory of God" (Rom 3:23 KJV).

The strength of every tree is in its roots. The deeper the roots in the soil, the more unshakeable the tree will be. It will withstand many storms as they come. Our founding fathers sowed deep roots of God into the country. Now, we as a new generation have elected, *chosen*, not to water that soil and pass it on to our children, and we are now bearing witness to the consequences of our actions. We have also been ignorant about the time and season we are in, unlike the sons of Issachar—the Hebrew men who understood the times and seasons and who knew what Israel should do.

It is written: "Of the tribe of Issachar, men who understood the times, with knowledge of what Israel should do, two hundred chiefs; and all their relatives were at their command…" (1 Chr 12:32 AMP).

Therefore, amid the pandemic, chaos, anarchy, frustrations, and demonstrations that are taking place in America, and all over the world, let us not lose site of the timing of these events. Yes, it is true that we are a few months away from choosing who will lead us in the next four years as our president. Equally important, we are also in a time and season that the Bible accurately predicted. We are currently witnessing the age of smartphones, iPads, and other electronic gadgets, as predicted by the prophet Daniel. Jesus, the Son of God, also spoke about these times we are in, and it is written in the Bible. We are very privileged to be seeing all of these things unfold in our midst. Many prophets and high priests from several thousand years ago would have loved to have witnessed what we are seeing today. We are not only in a political season that is noteworthy; we also live in a sinful world far worse than the times of the parents of this baby boomer generation. Yes, the number one reason for all of these unforeseen challenges we face today is sin. Remember this truth: Iniquity and rebellion against God open the door for Satan to unleash mayhem on any nation, or the entire world. Without sin in the "camp," Satan has no power over us. If you want to get a heads up on what is about to befall the earth, run to the closest Walmart to purchase a Bible, or order one from Amazon, and start reading it. You won't regret it. Read Matthew 24 and the book of Revelation.

It is written: "For then there will be great distress, unequaled from the beginning of the world until now—and never to be equaled again. 'If those days had not been cut short, no one would survive, but for the sake of the elect those days will be shortened" (Mt 24:21-22 NIV).

There is no perfect person on this earth. Without exception, we have all sinned and come short of the glory of God. Yet the Bible tells us that Hashem(God) sent the Messiah, Jesus Christ, who knew no sin because He never sinned, to become a sin offering for us so you and I could be reconciled with Him in heaven. Yes, God wants us *everyone* to walk in the righteousness He has already provided for us through His Son, Jesus Christ. We just have to acknowledge Him and receive His Son in our hearts. It is that simple. But you would be surprised how many are struggling to do this and are caught up in all kinds of deception today. After you become reborn, Jesus, through His Holy Spirit, will then work with you and help you shed the dead weight of the old

49

life you lived—the one you thought was fabulous—and He will usher you into a new life, where you will live according to His Word, in righteousness and holiness. Contrary to what people think or perceive in their hearts, God will not take away the fun from your life, except the things that could bring you long-term harm and put you outside His will. Jesus came to this world so that you can have life and live life abundantly.

Remember that the first miracle Jesus performed was at a wedding at Galilee in Cana. They ran out of wine, and this would have been a lifetime embarrassment for the wedding party. Jesus stepped in and turned water into wine. Hallelujah! It says it was the best wine that has ever been served at a wedding feast. Therefore, Jesus likes to party, too. If He is at your party, one thing is for sure: You won't run out of the nicest wine. Jesus, however, doesn't get drunk and become obnoxious; He considers this a sin. People who continuously engage in drunkenness and debauchery, to the point where their senses are dulled and it has taken over their lives, run the risk of arriving in the wrong place when they die and leave the earth. You know what I mean.

The blood of Jesus, which was shed on the cross of Calvary more than 2,000 years ago for you and me, cleanses us from all sins and makes us spotless in the eyes of God. Without this we are totally dependent on our own human efforts to be right-standing in the eyes of God and, above all, to make it to heaven. When you fully understand the holiness of God, you begin to recognize how it would be impossible to live right without believing right, and it would be an exercise in futility. Total failure! In fact, without the cleansing power of Jesus' blood, we all stand condemned to death. This is because we are, after all, imperfect human beings, and if we are to mirror our lives to what the Word of God says, you would be surprised how much we are in need of God's mercy because we come short of the glory of God.

50

It is written: "But God demonstrates his own love for us in this: While we were still sinners, Christ died for us" (Rom 5:8 NIV).

The sins of Adam and Eve, in a nutshell, placed a death sentence on us all. In fact, God told Adam that if he ate fruit from the tree of the knowledge of good and evil, he would surely die. Unfortunately, I am not sure Adam properly relayed that message to his helpmate, Eve. You would think such dire warnings from God Almighty would have deterred Adam from becoming ensnared in the disobedience Eve brought on herself by listening to the serpent instead of obeying her husband's instructions. Yet this was not the case, and Adam fell from grace. When they both ate the forbidden fruit, they died that day. You see, the Bible tells us that Adam lived 930 years. Therefore, you may say, "Hey, Peter, Adam did not die that day." However, don't forget that the time clock in heaven and on Earth are very different. One day in heaven is the equivalent to 1,000 years on Earth, as was mentioned by the disciple Peter in the Bible.

It is written: "But do not forget this one thing, dear friends: With the Lord a day is like a thousand years, and a thousand years are like a day" (2 Pt 3:8 NIV).

So you see, you do not have to be an expert in math to figure out that Adam actually died that day in heaven, and he was kicked out of the Garden of Eden. This is because he only lived 930 years. He never got to the 1,000 years that would have been the equivalent to one day in heaven. So this death sentence has been on mankind since then. We no longer live forever. This is why Christ came to redeem us, so that when we leave this earth, we will live forever. Hallelujah! We will never die again. That said, you and I want to make sure we are in the right place with Jesus. Living forever in the lake of fire is a very scary thought. Jesus came to deliver us from this second death sentence.

It is written: "Indeed, we felt we had received the sentence of death. But this happened that we might not rely on ourselves but on God, who raises the dead. He has delivered us from such a deadly peril, and he will deliver us again. On him we have set our hope that he will continue to deliver us..." (2 Cor 1:9-10 NIV).

In this world we live in, we see ourselves, in our best efforts, still struggling to live right. We have a hard time even obeying the simple instruction to love one another. Do we love each other and our neighbors the way God expects us to? Remember, Jesus set a high standard of love that we should all be emulating and putting into our actions and deeds if we are to remain part of Him. I am not even going to ask whether we love God with all our hearts, souls, and minds, because, quite frankly, very few people, even among Christians, have entered into this kind of relationship with God. In this dispensation we are in, our lives are often distracted with so many things that are unimportant when compared to our personal relationships with God. Unfortunately, these distractions and bunny trails are front and center in our lives, and we can't discern His voice when He is speaking to us.

These distractions include social media, texting, television, sports activities for the kids, entertainment of all kinds, happy hour, and everything else but God, until a pandemic like Covid-19 breaks out in the nation. Then we start calling on His name, or in arrogance we ask, "Where is God? How can this happen to us?" Really?! Nevertheless, God loves you, and His love for you is unconditional and constant. He cares for you and is your burden bearer. Permit me to make a suggestion. Let's put ourselves in God's shoes for once. Imagine you had a child, and all your child wanted to do was go to your neighbor's house or visit other places without you. The kid you brought into the world never wanted to spend time with you. The only time your child acknowledged you was when your child wanted something.

52

I know there are some children like that today in this world, and this is unfortunate. No parent should go through this ordeal. Forget about this kid greeting you in the mornings or say good night to you at night; this kid just ignores you. It wouldn't take long before you started getting concerned, especially if you carried that child for nine months or adopted the child at an early age. You would be frustrated with this kid and might grow to dislike the kid.

This is not so with God; instead, He will drop hints and signs around you telling you to come to Him and fellowship with Him through the Holy Spirit. God's love transcends human love because our Heavenly Father's love for us does not fluctuate like the stock market, even when we are naughty or outright disobedient. He made us, and it is hugely important to Him that we succeed in life and live a life that glorifies His name. He takes no delight in seeing us go through struggles that bring us unnecessary pain and discomfort, except when it will bring about a greater good and make us better people. Yet that is usually not His first choice for you and me.

It is our disobedience, more often than not, that puts us through trials. Yes, there are times when we are doing things right and will still go through some rough times. This happens when God wants to sharpen us spiritually and fortify us for the new heights we are about to climb to. It is often for God's elevation and to display His glory in your life. These exceptions are usually brief, and these testing times often lead to promotions tomorrow. Remember, it is the desire of the Father that not one person should perish. Yet we are born with the ability to make our own choices because our Father in heaven loves us so much that He gave us free will. He knew this free wheel would cause some of us to take the wrong paths in life because of our sinful nature and desires. He always has a plan to bring us back to Himself, but it is not done forcefully. Remember that God created you in His image, and so you are not a robot.

We need to graduate quickly from blaming God anytime there is a crisis in our lives or a pandemic in the world. We must look within. The world has opened so many doors for the enemy, the devil, to afflict us. Yet we have the power within us, through the Holy Spirit that takes residence in our hearts when we are reborn, to shut those doors, kick the devil out, and realign our lives once more with the one who sent His only begotten Son to die for us. Jesus is the same yesterday, today, and forever, and He is calling for us to be reconciled with one another in love. The topic of being reborn isn't new; it was taught by Jesus Himself from the onset of His ministry, and he was the one who made it a condition for anyone to enter into the kingdom of God, no exceptions. If you have an issue with this criteria Jesus set up, take it up with Him rather than contending, opposing, and fighting against those saints (God's people) who preach this truth. They have a mandate to preach the gospel until Christ returns.

There was a man named Nicodemus. He was a member of the Jewish ruling counsel, a Sanhedrin (the highest legal, legislative, and judicial body of the Jews), a highly respected teacher of the Old Testament, and a scholar in those days when Jesus began His ministry. Nicodemus was also a pharisee. He believed in the Messiah and the resurrection. He was very knowledgeable about the laws of Moses. He had been waiting for the Messiah, Jesus. Unlike other Pharisees, Nicodemus was fascinated by and captivated with Jesus. He had been spying on Jesus, trying to ascertain whether rabbi called Jesus was the real deal. Nicodemus was also very affluent and was believed to be the third richest man in all of Israel. He was a powerful man indeed. Most of his colleagues did not like Jesus, and they were very envious of how Jesus was pulling large crowds in through His bold preaching and authority over demons. Not Nicodemus, though. He just wanted to confirm what his heart was telling him: that this Jesus was the Son of God

54

Moses and the prophets had spoken about in times past. He would often go at night to meet with Jesus. One night he went to meet with Jesus, and the conversation went like this. It is written: "He came to Jesus at night and said, 'Rabbi, we know that you are a teacher who has come from God. For no one could perform the signs you are doing if God were not with him.' Jesus replied, 'Very truly I tell you, no one can see the kingdom of God unless they are born again.' 'How can someone be born when they are old?' Nicodemus asked. 'Surely they cannot enter a second time into their mother's womb to be born!' Jesus answered, 'Very truly I tell you, no one can enter the kingdom of God unless they are born of water and the Spirit. Flesh gives birth to flesh, but the Spirit gives birth to spirit. You should not be surprised at my saying, 'You must be born again'" (Jn 3:2-7 NIV).

You can see that Jesus mentioned three times that you must be born again. So take it seriously. You never know when your last minute will come. The words "born again" and "reborn" do not belong to the Pentecostal church, the non-denomination church, or the charismatic church, etc. They belong to Jesus, and it doesn't matter what kind of church you go to as long as you are born again and as long as that church believes that the Bible is the infallible Word of God and that even though men were the instruments God used, the Bible was inspired by the power of the Holy Spirit. They must also recognize that the Holy Spirit is a person and the central power on Earth as far as your spiritual work with God is concerned. He is the one God sent through His Son, Jesus Christ, to you. Without the Holy Spirit, you can do nothing on Earth. Many Christians are living frustrated lives because their church doesn't teach them about the Holy Spirit, who is a person. Even if you read your Bible, you need the Holy Spirit to interpret it for you so your understanding will be beneficial for you.

It is written: "Such confidence we have through Christ before God. Not that we are competent in ourselves to

55

claim anything for ourselves, but our competence comes from God. He has made us competent as ministers of a new covenant—not of the letter but of the Spirit; for the letter kills, but the Spirit gives life" (2 Cor 3:4-6 NIV).

Now it is also important that you run away from any church or preacher, regardless of titles or size, that dares to question the Word of God, because they are wrongfully questioning Jesus. Anyone who says it is wrong to believe or agree with everything written in the Bible is someone you shouldn't associate yourself with, lest they corrupt your thoughts and cause you to miss heaven. It was predicted many years ago that powerful people with influence would arise and question the Word of God, and we see this happening today. Bad company corrupts good morals. Many people have begun to water down the truth in the Word of God so that they can indulge in the things God frowns upon or rebel against God without their conscience pricking them. Truly, we are indeed about to enter into the last days.

It is written: "As it was in the days of Noah, so it will be at the coming of the Son of Man. For in the days before the flood, people were eating and drinking, marrying and giving in marriage, up to the day Noah entered the ark; and they knew nothing about what would happen until the flood came and took them all away. That is how it will be at the coming of the Son of Man" (Mt 24:37-39 NIV). Listen carefully: Trump and Biden will come and go; Beyoncé we come and go; Jay-Z will come and go; Tiger Woods will come and go; the Pope in Rome will come and go; Serena Williams will come and go; Anderson Cooper of CNN will come and go; Hannity and Laurel Ingram of Fox News will come and go; Rachel Meadow of NBC will come and go; the View will come and go; Oprah will come and go; Jeff Bezos of Amazon will come and go; Putin and Kim Jong-un of North Korea will come and go.

56

Even heaven and Earth will pass away, but the Word of God will stand forever. God has exulted His Word (the Bible) above His name, and Jesus is the Word in written form.

It is written: "In the beginning was the Word, and the Word was with God, and the Word was God. The same was in the beginning with God. All things were made by him; and without him was not anything made that was made" (Jn 1:1-3 KJV).

The pillar of Christianity is the infallible Word of God. It is the anchor of our faith. It opens us to the wonderful promises of God, at least to those who meditate on it day and night. It sets the moral compass for the whole Earth, because men would only put emphasis on what they like if it were left to them. It is for the rich as well as for the poor. There is a message for everyone under the sun. Its words never return to the earth void, and it always accomplishes what it says. The prophecies in the Bible are 98% fulfilled, making it the exception out of other religious books on Earth. It was inspired by the Holy Spirit, who was the same spirit who hovered over the waters before the creation of this earth. It is active, alive, and powerful, and it brings conviction to the soul and can heal the sick body.

Yes, many wealthy and affluent people believe erroneously that they can live their lives without acknowledging the God who made them rich. They forget that the Bible says God blesses the wicked and the righteous, and He causes the rain to fall on both the people who call on His name and the people who don't know Him or could care less. He still blesses those people. However, before you say it is unfair, there is a caveat here. God says He blesses those who don't know Him (the wicked) because their final destiny has already been determined. In other words, He will let them enjoy this Earth because after they die, it will be miserable for them. The worst thing a rich man can do is to never give credit to God Almighty for putting him in the position of wealth he is enjoying.

It is written: "Then Jesus said to his disciples, 'Truly I tell you, it is hard for someone who is rich to enter the kingdom of heaven. Again I tell you, it is easier for a camel to go through the eye of a needle than for someone who is rich to enter the kingdom of God.' When the disciples heard this, they were greatly astonished and asked, 'Who then can be saved?' Jesus looked at them and said, 'With man this is impossible, but with God all things are possible'" (Mt 19:23-26 NIV).

Now let me be crystal clear: Jesus wasn't saying a rich person cannot go to heaven or is not welcome. Nothing could be further from the truth. We know for a fact that many rich people have indeed gone up to heaven when they left the earth. What Jesus was saying and showing the disciples was that most people who are very rich do not think they have any need for God. And this is true. They often feel secured. They believe their lives are based on their net worth and possessions. They don't realize that true godliness with contentment is great gain and great wealth. Jesus underscores His message even further by telling a parable of a man who was so rich that he decided to store some of his money and grain in newly built barns, securing his assets for future use, then kicking back and relaxing. Surprisingly, Jesus referred to that man as a fool because this man, like many wealthy people today who have worldly riches, did not consider eternity (after life, when you live forever in the New Jerusalem or the lake of fire). He did not realize the one thing he did not have control over was what hour he would leave the earth. Ironically, that man was supposed to die that night and wasn't aware of it. And even worse, he had not taken part in God's Kingdom on Earth, helping the less fortunate and helping spread the gospel to the unreachable areas of the world.

58

It is written: "Then he told them a parable, saying, 'There was rich man whose land was very fertile *and* productive. And he began thinking to himself, "What shall I do, since I have no place [large enough in which] to store my crops?" Then he said, "This is what I will do: I will tear down my storehouses and build larger ones, and I will store all my grain and my goods there. And I will say to my soul, 'Soul, you have many good things stored up, [enough] for many years; rest *and* relax, eat, drink and be merry (celebrate continually).'" But God said to him, "You fool! This *very* night your soul is required of you; and *now* who will own all the things you have prepared?" So it is for the one who continues to store up and hoard possessions for himself, and is not rich [in his relationship] toward God'" (Lk 12:16-21 AMP).

Now, there are millions of affluent people who have passed away and gone unto glory to be with the Heavenly Father. These are the ones whose riches never superseded their faith and allegiance to God. They are also the ones who sowed the Word bountifully in God's Kingdom on Earth, and since no one can outgive God, He made them prosperous. It is better to be rich than to be poor because it is always better to give than to receive. God has put a conscience in every human heart. Each one of us, even if we say we do not believe in any religious deity or god, has a heart that has been wired to know the difference between right and wrong. Most adults know what is morally right and what is morally incomprehensible. Yet certain people's hearts can be so hardened that they never feel remorseful when they sin against God. I pray to the Father of our Lord Jesus Christ that you, the reader of this book, have a heart that will be sensitive to the Holy Spirit when He convicts you of certain things you should not be doing and brings to your remembrance who you are in Christ Jesus, empowering you to abstain from a sinful lifestyle.

It is written: "No temptation has overtaken you except what is common to mankind. And God is faithful; he will not let you be tempted beyond what you can bear. But when you are tempted, he will also provide a way out so that you can endure it" (1 Cor 10:13-14 NIV).

There is a group of people in America today who despise the things of God. These individuals and groups I am referring to are unfortunately very much in our midst. There is a growing number of people in our college campuses who are atheists. Thank God we have the Constitution, which allows them to be what they are. It is called freedom of religion. They are free to believe or not to believe. This is the beauty of America, and it is indeed what makes her a unique nation among many other nations. On the other hand, many of these erudite professors who have achieved tenure and are set financially for life falsely believe they do not need any help from the God of Abraham, Isaac, and Jacob. Many of them think God is just a myth. Some of them unfortunately go about teaching our kids that there is no God. They are knowingly religiously indoctrinating this generation of college kids. They tell them religion is for certain gullible people. They refer to people who believe in the Bible in its entirety as extremists, accusing them of being the bedrock of intolerance in our society. This is indeed very funny and ironic, as the most intolerant person by definition is the atheist who doesn't allow any acknowledgement of any god, regardless of his own lack of religion.

These individuals are disputing the truth that most of our founding fathers had a covenant with God. They are also teaching our kids that socialism is the best form of government, making reference to certain nations in Western Europe. They forget it was the Marshall Plan from America that rebuilt Europe after the Second World War. They forget it was the free market system that created a wealthy South Korea, and on the other hand, the socialist state, controlled by one man and a communist system, created a poverty-stricken North Korea. This spiritual virus they are feeding our kids is detrimental to our longterm economic security, because they are raising a generation of young adults who will not honor the God of their grandfathers, who made America prosperous. This is indeed a pity, and there is a need for collective repentance in our nation. They are caught up in themselves. They think that because they are smart, they are better than others. They wear a chip on their shoulder.

The only time they might think of God is when there is a disaster, such as 9/11 in 2001. Many of them were still wearing diapers when the twin towers in New York were hit by terrorists from Saudi Arabia. In fact, this, too, may mean nothing to them. After all, at the height of the Covid-19 pandemic, many of our young adults were still partying at the various beaches in America and were very reluctant to cancel their spring breaks. You will hear them say, "Oh, religion is for the vulnerable, the poor, or those who need some encouragement because of their lives of struggle." Yet it is this very young, aspiring generation that God longs to reintroduce to Himself, and He loves them. He knows many of them were never taught about things that pertain to God. If my parents had not gone to church, I would be just like them. Therefore, you cannot really blame them.

For it is written: "How, then, can they call on the one they have not believed in? And how can they believe in the one of whom they have not heard? And how can they hear without someone preaching to them? And how can anyone preach unless they are sent? As it is written: 'How beautiful are the feet of those who bring good news!'" (Rom 10:14-15 NIV).

Nevertheless, there is still a sizeable remnant of these young adults who are on fire for the Kingdom of God, and God has raised them up to proclaim Christ everywhere they go. I'll tell you the truth: No one—regardless of religion, wealth, power, status, or job—would, in their best human

61

effort, be able to make it to heaven without being reborn spiritually. This is true even if you are the kindest person on Earth; even if you give your hard-earned money to the poor, the sick, and the destitute; and even if you support more charitable causes than Bill Gates. Unfortunately, because of Adam and Eve's disobedience, we all carry the sin nature in our DNA, and so we will not be able to make it to heaven without the blood of Jesus. Unredeemed, sinful flesh cannot dwell in heaven. We all need a spiritual rebirth. We already went through physical birth, and that's why we are in this world. You need a glorified body to go to heaven, and this is only given to the reborn when they are raptured and the trumpet blast sounds in the sky. Let's look at it from a scientific perspective. Remember, Jesus was the only person that came to this earth who was not born through the sperm of a man.

Every other religious deity was born through the sperm of a man. Buddha was born through the sperm of a man, and so were Mohammed, Ramakrishna, Shinto, and all other religious figures of the past. Except one person, and His name is Jesus. Secondly, with all due respect to other faiths, let it be known that none of the above mentioned powerful religious figures had things written about them before they were born, but Jesus did. Jesus' birth was predicted with bullet point accuracy 800 years before He was born, and it was written in the scrolls, right down to where He would be born. Imagine something being written about you hundreds of years before you came to the earth. It is amazing. Now, remember, it is the sperm of the man that determines your blood type when you are born. For the sake of those who are not religious or have no relationship with the God of Abraham, Isaac, and Jacob, I will prove it scientifically, biologically, and genetically. It isn't rocket science. Besides, God invented science. Both science and genetics are subject to God. Anytime there is a custody battle in which the court is trying to determine who is the father of a particular child,

62

they are able to resolve the matter by simply carrying out a blood test.

Ironically, it is noteworthy and interesting that both the Koran, the Muslims' holy book, and the Bible testify to the truth that Mary, the mother of Jesus, was indeed a virgin, and she was overshadowed by the Spirit of God, became pregnant, and gave birth to a baby boy named Jesus. The Old Testament books (Tanakh), used by the Jews along with the first five books of Moses, accurately predicted that Jesus would be born from a virgin and that the city Bethlehem was where he would be born. It is important to note that, while Jesus was on Earth, He did not sin, and He went to his crucifixion without sinning. He had no unforgiveness in his heart. Anyone on Earth who is unforgiving instantly carries sin. If God forgives you for your sins, you ought to forgive those who hurt you, offended you, trespassed against you, gossiped about you, stabbed you in the back, or murdered your brother, sister, parents, relatives, etc. Holding grudges can prevent you from going to heaven, and it will establish a spirit of bitterness in your heart. This is in the Lord's Prayer, which is given to Christians, so you are without excuse. Jesus literally asked His Heavenly Father, Hashem, to forgive those who had brutally put Him through an excruciating crucifixion, which was the most horrific way to die, even by today's standard. Even worse, He was innocent of the crime He was accused of.

Now, my dear friends, you see where I am going here. We have all had some unforgiveness in our hearts at some point in our lives here on Earth. Sometimes people do offend us and hurt us. When Jesus was asking His Father to forgive the Roman soldiers who hurt Him physically, He used the first of His last seven words to ask God to forgive them. In other words, before you and I can come to the Father in prayer, first make sure, like Jesus, you have no unforgiveness in your heart. This means you have forgiven those who offended you. Is it easy? No, it is not. But Hashem, our

Father, insists we do so. Learn from the Master. His name is Master Jesus. His last words were recorded. He said, "It is finished..." (Jn 19:30 KJV). This meant He had fulfilled His mission on Earth. The number seven represents completion.

It is written: "From one man he made all the nations, that they should inhabit the whole earth; and he marked out their appointed times in history and the boundaries of their lands" (Acts 17:26 NIV). Adam was the first man God created. God loved Adam so much that He created a helpmate for Adam, and Adam named her Woman. She would later be known as Eve. The woman was created by God using one of Adam's ribs after putting Adam into a deep sleep. When he awoke, there was a gorgeous woman. None of the pageant winners of the Miss Universe and Miss World contests could compare to her. She was crowned Miss Heaven before Adam took her as his wife. She therefore had more wisdom than all the Miss Universe and Miss Worlds winners we have all witnessed on television, as Adam was full of God's wisdom.

They lived in a majestic Garden that was designed by the inalienable Creator, the Elohim Chayim (The Living God). Adam hung out with the all-powerful God of heaven and Earth. Needless to say, the late Albert Einstein and the most brilliant men on the earth paled in comparison to what Adam possessed.

Some of God's wisdom rubbed off on Adam just by hanging around with God and walking with Him in the cool of the night. I only wonder what they talked about. Adam named all the animals, birds, sea mammals, and plant species. He was the greatest zoologist and biologist ever known to man, and unlike Moses, he literally saw God face to face. Eve was God's personal gift to Adam. Adam was so mesmerized by her beauty and appearance that when he had a choice whether to obey God or not, Adam chose to go with her and disobey God, which had devasting consequences.

64

Both were immediately cast out of the Garden of Eden. We are all still paying the price today.

It is written: "So God drove the man out; and at the east of the Garden of Eden He [permanently] stationed the cherubim and the sword with the flashing blade which turned round and round [in every direction] to protect *and* guard the way [entrance, access] to the tree of life" (Gn 3:24 AMP).

Our redemption comes through a Jew called Jesus Christ.

It is written: "Therefore, just as sin entered the world through one man, and death through sin, and in this way death came to all people, because all sinned..." (Rom 5:12 NIV).

It is written: "Consequently, just as one trespass resulted in condemnation for all people, so also one righteous act resulted in justification and life for all people" (Rom 5:18 NIV).

It is written: "For just as through the disobedience of the one man the many were made sinners, so also through the obedience of the one man the many will be made righteous" (Rom 5:19 NIV). Through Jesus all are made righteous.

Remember that Satan is the father of sin. He has already been defeated by the blood of the lamb. Nevertheless, he goes around looking for those whom he may devour. His targets are individuals who are not grounded in the Word and who have not come to the knowledge that without Christ you perish. These individuals may go to church and celebrate Christmas and Easter, but they are not plugged into any church, and they do not give any of their hardearned money to worthy causes or a church. They may put a dollar in the offering basket and feel good about themselves, yet they are very rich. Sometimes they would rather gamble it away and lose it in the casinos. I am not saying you cannot go to Las Vegas to relax and shop and even lose a few dollars to see if you can win something. I am talking about an individual who loses thousands of dollars that he could have given to help the poor in Africa, to support a ministry doing God's work in Pakistan, or to support the 10/40 corridor, where many Christians risk their lives in the predominantly Islamic nations to preach the gospel. But this individual does nothing to advance God's Kingdom.

Then there are those who believe their human effort of goodness and service to the vulnerable in society gets them to heaven without them confessing or surrendering their life to Jesus. I used to be part of this group before I was reborn. I did not do drugs; I went to church every now and then. I was Catholic and prayed my rosary. So as far as I was concerned, I was the perfect candidate to go to heaven, even though I was fornicating. I knew that was a sin, but I did not care. I felt it was a passage in life and that it wasn't enough to disqualify me. In summary, I really thought I was good guy and not a bad person at all. Sound familiar? Have you, like me, referred to yourself as good when you are trying to justify why you should go to heaven when you die? But when I read this in the Bible after I was reborn, it was an eye opener for me.

It is written: "A certain ruler asked him, 'Good teacher, what must I do to inherit eternal life?' 'Why do you call me good?' Jesus answered. 'No one is good—except God alone" (Lk 18:18-19 NIV).

Jesus was simply saying that we should not depend on our goodness to get us to heaven. Jesus said that even He cannot say He was good, even though Jesus was without sin throughout His life on Earth. In my opinion, that is really good. However, Jesus answered the ruler this way in order to warn those who keep looking to themselves and what they have done, thinking that is what will get them to heaven, rather than looking to the Father and His Son, Jesus Christ. Yes, there are rewards for good deeds, but first you need to be reborn spiritually.

66

In the past, before I became a true believer, I asked God to forgive my sins, but I hadn't surrendered my heart to Him. So there was no willingness to repent. I felt I would miss out on the fun. I was even more in the wrong because I never acknowledged that Jesus had died for all my sins. Even worse, each time I was asked by passing evangelist, "How do you know you would be received in heaven if you died today," I would always pridefully talk about what I had done to be a good person. I didn't realize that Jesus came to this world to atone for our sins and that I couldn't get to heaven without Him. I knew that either Jesus was lying or I was the big liar. We could not both be right. I was very much being deceived by the devil. Oh, I knew there was a God and that there was heaven and hell, but I felt that if there was anyone qualified to be in heaven, it was me. I was full of myself, and I was no saint either. I lived a sinful lifestyle, except taking drugs. For some reason, drugs never appealed to me.

Thinking I was more qualified to make it to heaven than others just because of my kindnesses was a deception. This deception comes from Satan.

He is also the father of all liars on the earth. This was a title that was given to him by none other than Jesus Himself. Yes, lying is a sin in the eyes of God. This is why, as I said from the beginning, all have sinned and come short of the glory of God. Let me ask you a simple question: Have you ever told a lie? The short answer is yes. Everyone has at some point in their lifetime. We all told lies and exaggerated before being reborn. In this chapter I will point out many sins that are common today, not to judge anyone but to show how we perish without Christ. Some of the sins are so popular and ingrained in our culture today that to call it a sin can provoke anger and media backlash. Yet God has not changed, and His mighty power is very much alive to deal with anyone who persecutes His people for speaking the truth in a world led by Satan.

So, let's start discussing some of the common sins that many people do not know are sins. Remember, the purpose of this chapter is to underscore how all of us, in one way or another, have sinned against the all-powerful God of heaven and Earth, and even worse, we continue to sin. Sometimes we sin in ignorance. But ignorance is inexcusable and will not help you when you leave the earth. Exaggeration is a sin because it comes from the spirit of pride. Sometimes you exaggerate because it makes you feel good in the eyes of others, except there are those who know in their hearts that you are full of it. Unfortunately, not everyone is able to discern whether you are telling the truth or not. Exaggeration inflates one's ego. On the other hand, you may have lied in the past to cover up a crime for a friend. Sometimes you testify falsely in court, or sometimes you lie because you are afraid of the consequences if you told the truth. This happens often, especially if you are part of a street gang. Yet the Bible tells us that God has not given us a spirit to fear because fear is a powerful spirit of Satan); instead, God gives you love, a sound mind, and self-discipline.

Regardless, in the eyes of God, simply put, lying and exaggeration are sins, and you cannot justify sin before God. When Jesus was speaking with teachers of the law and certain Jews, informing them He did not come on His own but that God had sent Him to die for our sins, they did not believe Him. Jesus then told them indirectly that He was aware they wanted to kill Him, and it was in that conversation that Jesus referred to Satan as a murderer and the father of liars.

It is written: "You belong to your father, the devil, and you want to carry out your father's desires. He was a murderer from the beginning, not holding to the truth, for there is no truth in him. When he lies, he speaks his native language, for he is a liar and the father of lies" (Jn 8:44 NIV).

Jesus never likes to sugarcoat the truth. We all need to adopt this attitude instead of allowing progressive politics to influence our conversations with each other, masking the truth because we are worried it will offend someone. I want you to know that the sin of lying, whether you do it constantly or every once in a while, can be forgiven if you accept Jesus in your heart and ask Him to send the Holy Spirit to you so you can believe the right things and, as a result, live to please our Heavenly Father. We all live in a world that is starkly different from our parent's era. It is now sometimes more uncomfortable to tell the truth in situations that are considered sensitive in the society we live in. Even worse, it is more comfortable to conform to societies' desires and skate the truth in order to be accepted. The children of God are set apart by God Himself to stand their ground and speak truth in all matters. Do this even if you are ostracized by your peers and relatives, and Christ's light will shine on you. Above all, God Himself will defend and protect you.

When you have Christ in you, and the hope of glory, everything becomes much easier. Your language will change. You will no longer feel the desire to curse in your everyday conversations. People who can communicate without having to curse come across as individuals who have learned to discipline their tongues. The Word of God frowns on crass language. When you are reborn, your perception will also change. You will have the mind of Christ. You will become more aware of what people say, and you will be sensitive to the direction of the Holy Spirit. Being reborn is more than just a confession. It is the regeneration of your entire being. You are entering into a new citizenship, and that is the citizenship of heaven. You do not necessarily renounce your earthly citizenship, but you allow God's Word to guide your everyday decisions on Earth. This is hugely important because you are only on this earth for a short period of time. Eternity has no limitation, and you want to make sure you are going to the right place when you take your last breath.

Another reason it is critical to be reborn is that certain invisible things take place. Among the most important is you being washed in the blood of Jesus. The reason why this is critical is because of Satan. He is a superb attorney and is the accuser of you and me. The only attorneys smarter than the devil are Jesus, the Holy Spirit, and, of course, the Father in heaven. For the servant will never be greater than his master. It's profoundly interesting to point out that the Bible refers to both the Holy Spirit and Jesus (Yeshua) as the advocate. The Holy Spirit is your advocate on Earth, and Jesus is your advocate in heaven. They are also both referred to as the truth. Jesus is the Way, the Truth, and the Life (Jn 14:6), and the Holy Spirit is the spirit of truth (Jn 15:26). One is in heaven, and one is on earth.

It is written: "'When the Advocate comes, whom I will send to you from the Father—the Spirit of truth who goes out from the Father—he will testify about me" (Jn 15:26 NIV). and in the book of first John in the new testament Jesus is referred to as the advocate.

It is written: "My dear children, I write this to you so that you will not sin. But if anybody does sin, we have an advocate with the Father—Jesus Christ, the Righteous One. He is the atoning sacrifice for our sins, and not only for ours but also for the sins of the whole world" (1 Jn 2:1-2 NIV).

These two profound Scriptures send a very definitive message to the whole wide world. Number one: Truth is found in Jesus. Number two: He is the only one who can silence the accuser of you and me, and that accuser is Satan. In the book of Romans, it says that Jesus is forever making intercessions on behalf of you and me. Why does He do this? He loves us dearly, and Satan goes up there to accuse us of our sins.

Even Jesus warned the disciples to be wise as a serpent and harmless as a dove before He sent them out to preach the gospel. God is the Chief Justice and the fairest judge in the heavens and on Earth. As they say in Africa, "Jehovah has the final say." He is also the ultimate judge and has made Jesus judge of ALL. Once He decides on your case, no

70

one can go to any appellate court to file a motion to appeal Jesus' decision. Yet I have great news for you. God is faithful and keeps His commitment to those who put their faith in Him, and His justice is as deep as the oceans.

It is written: "Your loving kindness *and* graciousness, O LORD, extend to the skies, Your faithfulness [reaches] to the clouds. Your righteousness is like the mountains of God, Your judgments are like the great deep" (Ps 36:5-6 AMP).

Satan knows the God of Abraham, Isaac, and Jacob (Israel) more than any one of us living today. After all, before he fell from glory, he was the Chief Archangel and one who worshiped the Lord. Unlike you and me, he was not made from the dust of the earth. He was made by God from precious jewels. He was described as a very beautiful being, magnificent and full of wisdom. So he is shrewd even though he fell from grace.

It is written: "'You had the full measure of perfection *and* the finishing touch [of completeness], Full of wisdom and perfect in beauty. 'You were in Eden, the garden of God; Every precious stone was your covering: The ruby, the topaz, and the diamond; The beryl, the onyx, and the jasper; The lapis lazuli, the turquoise, and the emerald; And the gold, the workmanship of your settings and your sockets, Was in you. They were prepared On the day you were created" (Ez 28:12-13 AMP).

I can only imagine how gorgeous Satan was before the Fall. This information comes from the writings of Ezekiel, the Jewish prophet who had more visitations from God than any known prophet in the Tanakh (the Old Testament), apart from Moses, who saw the back of God and had God's hand cover his face so he would not die when He saw God's face. We also learn from this Scripture that Satan hung around in the Garden before Adam and Eve were created and placed there.

It is written: "And there was war in heaven: Michael and his angels fought against the dragon; and dragon fought

71

and his angels, And prevailed not; neither was their place found any more in heaven" (Rv 12:7-8 KJV).

It is written: "And war broke out in heaven, Michael [the archangel] and his archangels waging war with the dragon. The dragon and his angels fought, but they were not strong enough *and* did not prevail, and there was no longer a place found for them in heaven. And the great dragon was thrown down, the age-old serpent who is called the devil and Satan, he who *continually* deceives *and* seduces the entire inhabited world; he was thrown down to the earth, and his angels were thrown down with him" (Rv 12:7-9 AMP).

The beauty of the devil's body got to his head, and he became prideful, wanting to ascend the throne of heaven and take God's position. He fell and was cast down to the earth, along with one third of the angelic host in heaven. These fallen angels joined Satan in his suicide mission against God. I really wonder what he was thinking when he tried to plan a coup against God Almighty. He forgot who discerns the thoughts of man from afar. Remember, pride comes before destruction, and a haughty spirit comes before a fall. There is a saying in America that I like, and it goes like this: "Fool me once, shame on you. Fool me twice, shame on me." In other words, I should have learned my lesson the first time. There is a nice twist to this saying, and it is why we human beings are made from the dust of the earth.

Now, I am not in any way saying this is in the Bible, but I am wondering whether that's why God made you and me from clay, the dust of the earth, even though He created us in His own image. He did not throw in lapis lazuli, nor did He make our thoracic cage out of emeralds, nor did He build our lungs with twenty-four carat gold so they would be immune to the Coronavirus. We were designed differently. In His infinite wisdom, God did something even better. Even though we are made of flesh and blood, He created us in His image spiritually, and He gave us the Word of God to redeem us, sustain us, and direct us while we are on Earth.

72

When we leave this earth, we will have a glorified body like His.

It is written: "Then God said, 'Let us make mankind in our image, in our likeness, so that they may rule over the fish in the sea and the birds in the sky, over the livestock and all the wild animals, and over all the creatures that move along the ground.' So God created mankind in his own image, in the image of God he created them; male and female he created them" (Gn 1:26-27 NIV).

Another powerful reason why we must be reborn and not allow religion to hinder salvation is because of how we think or perceive things that come into our minds. Even our thoughts can cause us to sin against God. The devil first thought about ascending God's throne, and he allowed it to fester in his heart until he finally tried to act on it. For us here on Earth, one sinful thing we do often is blame God for every problem that exists in the world. This includes say things like, "How can this terrible thing happen if there is a God?" Yet the above-mentioned biblical verse says God put us in charge and gave us power to rule over everything on Earth. So, if you see something like domestic terrorism or police brutality taking place and you hate what you observed, do something about it rather than pointing fingers to the one who gave you dominion power to rule the earth. Some do not even vote, and yet they are blaming God for everything.

Remember, God is the only one who can discern the thoughts of man and all spiritual beings. He is the omniscient God, the all-knowing God. While it is okay to admire beauty anywhere you see it, whether it is fruit or the physical appearance of a particular person, your admiration must not lead to you having thoughts of that person that are immoral in nature, as this is the sin of lust. Having negative thoughts toward anyone out of envy or hatred is a sin, but God is ready to forgive these sins through His Son, Jesus Christ. What, then, is not sin? I am sure you are asking this question. The answer is anything that is true, right, just, pure, admirable, lovely, excellent, or praiseworthy in the eyes of God. Even born-again Christians have yet to walk with the above-mentioned attributes 24/7. It is impossible as long as you live in this world. Nevertheless, with God all things are possible, and Jesus sent the Holy Spirit to teach us to enter into those things that glorify God's name. We will be like Jesus when we meet Him face to face. Until then, we must cooperate with the Holy Spirit, which will conform us physically into Christ's image and character. Do not look for perfection in this age; strive to allow the Holy Spirit, your advocate and caretaker on Earth, to transform you into becoming Christ's light on earth. Hallelujah.

I included this chapter to explain that all of us, without exception, have sinned and need redemption, as the penalty for sin, according to the Bible, is death. This rule was established thousands of years ago. The death written about here is eternal separation from God. Before Christ came to the earth, the law — as written about in the Torah, the first five books of the Bible — actually sent people to death physically for certain sins, one being adultery. That is behind us now because of the grace that was given to us. However, if you are not reborn, you risk spending your afterlife in the lake of fire.

I tell you the truth: Saying you are not a Christian, that you do not believe in the Bible, and that you have a different religion doesn't change God's mind about what is written in His Word, nor does it invalidate His existence. The excuse will be useless when you appear at the great white throne of judgment. Even as I write this, it is kind of uncomfortable for me, but I must let you know this truth. God would hold me accountable if I did not tell you, in plain language, what I was called to do. "Do not sugarcoat the gospel," I am reminded as I write this paragraph, so I am trying to be as plainspoken as possible so I do not enter into God's judgment myself. Ezekiel was a Jewish prophet of God, and he was used powerfully by God before he died in 570 BC.

74

Ezekiel was in Babylon because God gave Israel to King Nebuchadnezzar of Babylon due to their disobedience. Israel was invaded by a foreign army as a punishment from God, and America is following in a similar path. Yes, no nation today can withstand the military might of the United States, nor can they invade our country, but God has other ways of unraveling our greatness. This is what God told Ezekiel.

It is written: "'Son of man, I have made you a watchman for the people of Israel; so hear the word I speak and give them warning from me. When I say to a wicked person, "You will surely die," and you do not warn them or speak out to dissuade them from their evil ways in order to save their life, that wicked person will die for their sin, and I will hold you accountable for their blood. But if you do warn the wicked person and they do not turn from their wickedness or from their evil ways, they will die for their sin; but you will have saved yourself. 'Again, when a righteous person turns from their righteousness and does evil, and I put a stumbling block before them, they will die. Since you did not warn them, they will die for their sin. The righteous things that person did will not be remembered, and I will hold you accountable for their blood. But if you do warn the righteous person not to sin and they do not sin, they will surely live because they took warning, and you will have saved yourself'" (Ez 3:17-21 NIV). Every Jew who has been educated about Jewish history knows the story of when the Southern Kingdom of Israel was invaded by Nebuchadnezzar and, as a result, why many of its citizens were exiled in Babylon for seventy years. This is not fiction. Ask Diane Feinstein, the Sr. Senator from California. Ask Chuck Schumer, the Sr. Senator from New York. Ask Wolf Blitzer from CNN. They are Jews, and they can verify what I have written about the Jewish exiles in Babylon. They may not agree with me that Yeshua is the Messiah who came in the past and is coming again (that's the Word of the Holy

75

Spirit), but they will validate what I have written in this book about Ezekiel and the Jewish exiles in Babylon.

Now is the time for all of us, without exception, to be reconciled with this immortal, invisible, allpowerful God of heaven and Earth. I plead with all of you reading this book to turn to God now and be saved before it is too late. How many people died of Covid-19 without taking care of their eternal salvation? Life can be unpredictable for even the most meticulous and organized person. Repent (change your mindset) and seek the face of the one true God while there is still time. God will forgive everything and anything except blasphemy against the Holy Spirit. Whatever struggles you have, God will help you overcome them if you will follow Him. You do this by asking God to help you, and He will help you.

I remind you again: We are all sinners in need of salvation from the one true God through His Son, Jesus Christ. Let me give you another example that many have overlooked but that has severe ramifications as far as your eternal salvation is concerned. If you have hatred for a sibling, a friend, your parents, or men in authority because of a quarrel between you, you have sinned. It doesn't matter if you are the aggrieved one and that person is the guilty one in your own eyes. God expects you to reconcile with that family member as soon as you can. If you can't, God expects you to forgive them in your heart by praying for them and blessing them through your prayers. This means you should not often be recalling what they did to you in the first place. So, you see my point. We have again all sinned in one way or another, and we indeed come short of God's glory.

It is written: "Whoever claims to love God yet hates a brother or sister is a liar. For whoever does not love their brother and sister, whom they have seen, cannot love God, whom they have not seen" (1 Jn 4:20 NIV).

Remember, sin is anything that God dislikes or hates, anything He is known to sometimes punish people or

76

destroy cities or nations for. The old covenant points out the truth in the New Testament about how we have all come short of the glory of God. The New Testament spells out that it is the saving grace of Jesus Christ, through His death and resurrection, that makes us whole and right-standing with God forever. Unforgiveness, adultery, same sex marriage (although legal by law in America), greed, bitterness, murder, gossip, cheating on your taxes, anger, doing drugs, and getting drunk are sins because you do not own your body; God owns your body. Sin is sin in the eyes of God. No sin is worse than the other, even though certain sins tend to provoke His wrath.

A big sin is testifying against an innocent man. Many juries in the courthouses of America have sent many innocent people to jail. It hurts God to see people incarcerated for crimes they did not commit. Many of these people are from minorities, because racist juries have sent them to jail unjustly. Now, if you are one of those jurists who knowingly sent the wrong person to jail, why should God allow you to enter into heaven when you leave this world? You must repent and ask for forgiveness. If you are bold enough, confess publicly to what you did. If not, Satan will be right there to accuse you when your body goes to the grave, and your soul and spirit, which have just as much feeling as your physical body, will stand before the judgment throne of God. Many years ago I watched a 60-minute documentary about a young man who was wrongly convicted and sentenced to jail. While he was in jail, he was sexually molested and raped several times. He contracted full-blown aids, and later they found out he was innocent of the charges that led him to jail in the first place. He was then released. This hurt my heart. What was so powerful was that he was not bitter. The members of the jury that convicted him must repent before God and become reborn, or else they will not enter the Kingdom of heaven when they depart from the earth.

Anger is a sin that is committed by each one of us all too often, especially if it lingers on for over half a day. The Bible tells us we must not let the sun go down with anger in our hearts. This simply means that if you allow anger toward anyone fester and take root in your heart, you give Satan permission to trouble your life. You have a right to be angry, and even God gets angry, but not for long. There are cases in the Bible when Jesus was angry. Jesus hates injustice and hypocrisy, and during His time on the earth, He often expressed His moral outrage at unjust and hypocritical people. One such case was when Jesus wanted to heal a man with a shriveled hand on the sabbath, and in those days the Pharisees and Sadducees (High Priests) who lorded over the Jews felt Jesus should not make the man's hand whole. It was ridiculous. They were so religious that they had no love and never walked in love. Yet Jesus knew they would take their camels to the well to get water regardless of whether it was the sabbath or not.

God has a very long rope. In fact, I am convinced He has the longest rope in the world. It takes a long time for Him to begin passing judgment on a nation or a person who flouts His principles and laws. Yet nothing separates us from God more than rebellion against His chosen plan for our lives. God is very gentle, and He does not force Himself on you. You will always have a choice to make. You will always be free to ignore His wise counsel when it registers in your heart. Around sixty years ago, many of the sexual sins God hates were not in widespread practice in America. When the sexual revolution began in the 60s, it was championed as the right of individuals, particularly women, to do as they saw fit with their bodies. The desire then, and even now, was emancipation from religious doctrine and moral standards that had been passed on from one generation to another for years. They felt it was unfair for men to be able to have several partners when women were not allowed to. This campaign for freedom of the body began to grow and rise

78

in popularity, and God tended to overlook it because it was mostly limited to the hippies, although He was not happy about it. The Holy Scriptures have many stories about how this sin caused Israel to stumble so many times and lose favor with God. Devout Jews who practice their faith know what I am writing about. His avid hatred for this sin is because He created us in His image. What was seen as a noble idea to a few at that time has become a norm today in many parts of the world, and it started first in America. God still forgives this sin, like He does with many other sins. There are not many of us who can say we haven't violated God's statutes in this area, and I am not one of those who can. It was the grace of God that kept me from bringing a child into the world before marriage. But the hippies forgot one thing that is written in the Holy Scriptures.

It is written: "Do you not know that your bodies are temples of the Holy Spirit, who is in you, whom you have received from God? You are not your own; you were bought at a price. Therefore honor God with your bodies " (1 Cor 6:19-20 NIV).

Today, many nations in the world are adopting this lifestyle, and it is actually rare to find people waiting till they are married to bring a child into the world. The undermining of the family unit has had a devasting effect on the structured order of our nation. For example, you have some young women and men who have chosen to compromise and live with each other for years without the man ever putting a ring on her finger, and thus they are never committed to each other. The couples think it is okay, but what they do not realize is that either one of them can walk out of the relationship. This has happened all too many times, always to the detriment of the one who wanted a real commitment. God wants to help women in America by telling them that if you wait for the right person and don't immediately jump into bed with him, you will get more commitment from the man, and you won't have given up the most precious thing you have. This has been devastating to the inner cities and the economy in our nation. We no longer talk about it these days because of possible backlash from the media, who, in their drive to push a progressive agenda, often do more harm than good by obscuring the truth. Now, there has been great progress in the last three years. Unemployment among minorities prior to Covid-19 was the lowest in a generation, and programs initiated by Ivanka Trump helped many single mothers return to work by helping with the burdensome cost of childcare. Before Covid-19, ten million Americans were taken out of the welfare program. I do not care who gets the credit, but this was great news.

God is a merciful and caring Father. He knows there is indeed a generation of Americans who are unfortunately unaware that sex outside the marriage covenant, and giving birth to a child out of wedlock, is sin in the eyes of God. That is why I was ordered to include this truth in this book. This truth will set you free from deception, and it might prevent you, or others, from wrecking your future. I don't know about you, but most men do not like to be harassed to pay child support for a child not living with them. Unfortunately, there are other unintended consequences of sex out of wedlock, one being the number of pregnancies that have been aborted. God wants to change hearts rather than overturn a law. He knows that if the hearts of the people are not in line with the law of the land, they won't even keep the law in place if it is changed. An overturned law wouldn't last long; it would only be overturned again by another generation or political party that has the majority in Congress and, above all, controls the White House. He wants to change hearts in this nation to His perfect will.

Here is one more secret millions of Americans are currently unaware of. This secret has been imparted to me by the Spirit of God and by God's grace alone. So I am certainly not taking any credit. Now, pay attention. I have been privileged to know, along with others among the followers of Jesus Christ, that anytime innocent blood is shed, whether through murder or through abortion, it empowers Satan and his kingdom on Earth. Satan is then able to bring about all manner of trials and tribulations. Cities and nations will struggle to see economic vitality because of the innocent blood crying out to God for vengeance. It also gives Satan power to unleash other trials on the nation, such as some we are witnessing today.

In 2009, I worked with several pastors in North Minneapolis, where George Floyd was murdered, to bring about a spiritual revival that involved repentance and healing of the land, seeking forgiveness for the innocent blood shed on that soil due to drugs, prostitution, and gang violence. It was hard work, and the forces going against us in the realms of the spirit were strong. Also, North Minneapolis was inhabited many years ago by Jews, and some of the black churches used to be synagogues. When a riot broke out in North Minneapolis, many Jewish businesses were vandalized and destroyed. The Jews left, and the blacks took over their synagogues. They have to ask for forgiveness for that sin against the Jews. Much progress was made as I worked with the pastors in North Minneapolis, but we were far from finishing the work when I moved to Texas to embark on a new journey in life. From a spiritual perspective, I was the least surprised when the uprising we are seeing today broke out in North Minneapolis.

We do not, as a nation, get to choose the physical consequences of our actions, and there will be consequences even though God forgives us because He loves us. Today, many Americans, and millions more all over the world, have had sex before marriage, therefore engaging in sexual sin. To many people in the world, sex before marriage—or fornication, as it is called in the Holy Scriptures—is just part of life and is no big deal. Yet nothing could be further from the truth as far as God is concerned. Who am I to comment when I did not have an innocent past? I get it. I hear you

81

when you say, "Stop being a moral policeman." But the Bible lists sexual sin as one of the worst sins because it is more than just physical; it is spiritual, a sin against your own body. It degrades the human body spiritually, and portrays women, who were created in the image of God, as sex objects to men. However, women have other great attributes that should be recognized and appreciated. God does not like it when women are not loved or valued in the world in the same way He loves and values them.

It is hard for me to write about sexual sins because I sinned in this way before I was reborn. I did not know any better then, and I regret it. God said I should put it in the book, so I am writing about it. God says it is this sin that has opened many doors to Satan, allowing him to wreck the lives of many people in the world. America is looked up to by many nations, and whatever America does will be seen throughout the world. So it goes without saying that we have taught the world to engage in a lot of things that they did not engage in many years ago. Our lifestyle is emulated in many parts of the world. When pandemics are coming to the nations of the world, how can you expect divine protection from God when you are engaging in what He hates? Just think about it for a second. I do not know of any parent who rewards a disobedient child, therefore encouraging the child to continue being disobedient and rebellious. God's love for us does not negate His responsibility as a caring Father to correct us when we are wrong or out of order. There are challenging times coming to the earth, and all of us will need some divine protection to be immune. You cannot expect divine protection when you live a life of decadence and constant disobedience. Going to church without changing your mindset cannot help you. God is willing to work with you and empower you to live a life that has already been paid for by His Son. He is a patient God and will guide you step by step until you obtain the physical victory over all these iniquities.

All of these sins can be forgiven if you come to God through His Son, Jesus Christ, and have a spirit of repentance. Your sins were already atoned for. Even masturbation, although psychologists say it is good for you every once in a while, is a sin. The sperm of a man is a seed in the eyes of God. The Bible talks about how He killed a man for wasting his seed through this act that is now so common among men and women throughout the world. Addiction to this sin can be very strong, and that is why psychologists often say it is normal. Remember, even the air the psychologists breathe was made by God. God loves you dearly and unconditionally, but He considers this action a sin. It can open the door to unclean spirits and lead to other sins. Remember, our loving Father in heaven paid for all of our sins not in money or the blood of animal, none of which could forgive your sins; He paid with the blood of His only begotten Son. Therefore, we have a moral obligation to honor God with our bodies by abstaining from lust, and immorality.

Also, oppressing the poor, or taking advantage of the poor in any way, is a sin. Refusing to help someone when you can is considered selfish and is also a sin.

My point is that everyone on Earth has sinned and come short of the glory of God. We all do things we should not do, and we don't always do the things we should do, such as confessing our sins before God. Sometimes we do not do it because we think our sins are normal, and we have an "everyone does this" mentality. I don't point out the sins to condemn you. This is to show you that without asking forgiveness for these sins and being reborn, you cannot make it to heaven.

We are all praying for God's spirit to come upon the earth, shake that which needs to be shaken, and strengthen that which needs to be strengthen in our lives. Because you and I live in this fallen world and perverse generation. Once you are reborn, God expects you to embrace the freedom He provides for you and begin to live a life relatively free from the sins that entangled you in the past. It is not an overnight thing, and you will still fall from time to time as you learn to obey the Holy Spirit, who immediately takes residence in your heart. Paul of Tarsus, who wrote chapter seven of Romans—a must-read for newly reborn Christians—explains the battle that ensued the moment he became aware of his sins.

The New Testament will help you become Christcentered rather than sin conscious. If you go back to those sinful ways, you run the risk of becoming enslaved by that sin again. If it is an addiction, and if that sin has a demonic element, your condition will be worse than what it was before you were free. No one in their right mind wants to be a slave to anything. Therefore, you must press on by meditating on God's Word after you have been made clean by God's power. If you slip up, ask for forgiveness, and God will instantly forgive you because you are now reborn. That said, you want to develop a heart of repentance (NOT GOING BACK TO YOUR OLD WAY OF LIFE). Learn to say no to your flesh, or say, "Holy Spirit, help me," and the urge will go away.

God knows that the world we live in today makes it tough to abandon a sinful lifestyle without the help of the Holy Spirit. Temptations are everywhere and are sometimes knocking on your door. What God wants you to do today is recognize the futility of trying to live right and make it to heaven without giving your life to Christ. Right believing leads to right living. Believe in the Lord, Jesus Christ, and you shall be saved.

Another big sin is when you are a politician in power in Washington D.C. and you tell the truth under oath on camera in a conference committee (not available to the public), but when you are in public and not under oath, you lie to push a false narrative. You do this even though you know it would further divide our nation and increase animosity among

84

citizens, threatening the unity of our nation. It is a sin in God's eyes. And God hates this because it separates people and friends.

It is written: "For God so loved the world that he gave his one and only Son, that whoever believes in him shall not perish but have eternal life. For God did not send his Son into the world to condemn the world, but to save the world through him. Whoever believes in him is not condemned, but whoever does not believe stands condemned already because they have not believed in the name of God's one and only Son. This is the verdict: Light has come into the world, but people loved darkness instead of light because their deeds were evil" (Jn 3:16-19 NIV).

Jesus, our Savior, will be returning as the righteous judge of all flesh, and He has to hear both sides of the case. So, if you did not give your life to Christ, what case would you be able to make that would justify your entrance into the city of the living God? Even in the world we live in, a judge has to hear from the persecutor and the defense before rendering judgment. Again, God is sending message in this book for all of us to be reconciled with him while there is still time to do so. Do not look at your religion. If you think you can make it to heaven on your own volition and effort, it is because you do not understand the holiness of God.

It is written: "As God's co-workers we urge you not to receive God's grace in vain. For he says, 'In the time of my favor I heard you, and in the day of salvation I helped you'" (2 Cor 6:1-2 NIV).

Jesus is asking you to come as you are, and He will receive you. Do not resist the pull of the Holy Spirit in your heart. Come even if you are dirty mentally, physically, and spiritually. Surrender your life to Christ. Ask your church to baptize you in the name of the Father, Son, and Holy Spirit. Get a Bible and feed yourself with God's Word, because you are going to need it. It is a living book, powerful and active.

It is written: "But God showed his great love for us by sending Christ to die for us while we were still sinners" (Rom 5:8 NLT).

Ask any rabbi or scholar about the Tanakh (Old Testament), and they will tell you there is no way to measure God's holiness. Our own righteousness is like filthy rags to Him. The Jewish people devoted to their faith, Judaism, tend to understand the holiness of God quite well, sometimes even better than non-Jews. They know their founding fathers had to make animal sacrifices to atone for their sins. This had to be done often. And even the high priest had to atone for his own sins in those days. When Jesus died, the veil in the temple that leads to the Holy of Holies was torn to pieces. There was no longer a need for animal sacrifice, as the Son of God had become the sacrificial Lamb of God. Descendants from Israel had witnessed the wrath of God when they sinned against God corporately (as a whole nation). Israel had been invaded several times because of sin in the land, when they showed their unwillingness to repent even though God gave them ample time and opportunity to do so. The Northern Kingdom was invaded by the Assyrians, and they scattered all over Europe and Russia. The Southern Kingdom—its capital being Judah—was invaded by the Babylonians under King Nebuchadnezzar. According to historical records, even the pagan leader of Babylon, upon invading Israel, asked the Jewish leaders why they did not obey their God. In other words, he was saying, "Are you out of your mind? Don't you know how powerful your God is?" King Nebuchadnezzar knew that he could never have successfully invaded southern Israel if not for God's power. God hates corporate sin to this day.

A corporate sin is a sin practiced and sanctioned into law by the whole nation and its government. To hold a festival to celebrate a sin tends to get God more upset than just individuals struggling with sin. It is like thumbing a noses at Him.

86

Israel then would not repent for worshiping idols and doing detestable things despite God giving them several warnings through His prophets on the ground. But even the high priest, who was supposed to set an example by teaching God's law, was doing otherwise. Many times God's prophets were persecuted for telling the king of Israel the truth. Jeremiah was put in a cistern, which is like a well. So, when the invasion came, God's people were protected, but the disobedient rulers either lost their lives or were enslaved by the invading power. In these modern times, no country can successfully invade America. Yet God can bring down a nation anytime it celebrates what God calls a testable sin. America risks no longer being the number one superpower if her people don't repent and renounce corporate sins. It may take years, but it will surely come to pass because God does not change. The reborn will always be protected, but being reborn has nothing to do with going to church or being a pastor. You can't fool God with titles. He sees everything. This truth was revealed when Mary, the mother of Jesus, prophesied about this after going to Judea to see her cousin Elizabeth while carrying Yeshua (Jesus) in the womb.

It is written: "His mercy extends to those who fear him, from generation to generation. He has performed mighty deeds with his arm; he has scattered those who are proud in their inmost thoughts. He has brought down rulers from their thrones but has lifted up the humble. He has filled the hungry with good things but has sent the rich away empty. He has helped his servant Israel, remembering to be merciful to Abraham and his descendants forever, just as he promised our ancestors" (Lk1:50-55 NIV). What has changed since then? The animal sacrifices are no longer relevant because Jesus was the ultimate sacrifice. God's only Son is better than the sacrifice of bulls and rams. Yet the grace dispensation we are all in has never been a license to continue in habitual sin. Remember that God sent a plague among His own people in the past, and only those who

87

did not have hearts of deliberate and overt rebellion were protected. The grace and truth that come with Jesus Christ are the powers given to all of us through the Holy Spirit, helping us embrace the spirit of repentance and live a life worthy of God's Kingdom.

It is written: "For if it were otherwise, would not these sacrifices have stopped being offered? For the worshipers, having once [for all time] been cleansed, would no longer have a consciousness of sin. But [as it is] these [continual] *sacrifices* bring a fresh reminder of sins [to be atoned for] year after year, for it is impossible for the blood of bulls and goats to take away sins. Therefore, when Christ enters into the world, He says, 'SACRIFICE AND OFFERING YOU HAVE NOT DESIRED, BUT [instead] YOU HAVE PREPARED A BODY FOR ME [to offer]; IN BURNT OFFERINGS AND *sacrifices* FOR SIN YOU HAVE TAKEN NO delight. 'THEN I SAID, "BEHOLD I HAVE COME TO DO YOUR WILL, O GOD—[TO FULFILL] WHAT IS WRITTEN OF ME IN THE SCROLL OF THE BOOK'" (Heb 10:2-7 AMP).

God demonstrated this to the Jews by sending someone Moses had spoken about 2,000 years before He arrived on the scene to atone for the sins of the whole world. This is why, when Jesus was establishing who He was to the teachers of the law, He often referred to Moses.

It is written: "But do not think I will accuse you before the Father. Your accuser is Moses, on whom your hopes are set. If you believed Moses, you would believe me, for he wrote about me. But since you do not believe what he wrote, how are you going to believe what I say?" (Jn 5:45-47 NIV). For the consequence of sin is death, but the gift of God is eternal life.

I also have a message for my Jewish brothers and sisters whose descendants were the first fruit of our salvation and the ones whom God used to minister the gospel to us, the gentiles. I genuinely love God's special people because without them there would be no Christianity today. They are the root of our religion. My love for them is based on the fact that they remain God's special people to this day. Secondly, they were very helpful to my late father when he was a student in England and did not have much. He told me to always support the Jews. God has called each one of us to love one another, for this is indeed a great commandment. Based on the abovementioned and highlighted Scripture, which was written by Jews, the Messiah is telling the Pharisees and Sadducees of the 21st century—the ones who have not come to recognize that He is the Messiah— by saying Moses will be their accuser. Remember, everything written in the Bible so far, with the exception of a few things in book of Revelation, has come to pass with bullet point accuracy. And this book was written by Jews. Therefore, it means that there are some Jews who, according to the Bible, will be accused by Moses, who will be at the great white throne of judgement, for not recognizing Yeshua as the Son of God.

The good news here is that there will be no Christians there to accuse them. Thank God. I say this because many Jews have suffered under so-called Christians, and we know that the Catholic Church under the Vatican was passive during the genocide of the Jews by Hitler. The Vatican saved many Jews in Italy from the gas chamber, but they could have done far more to have altered this terrible chapter in the world. When I leave this world, the only person who will accuse me is the devil, and he will be silenced by Jesus because of the blood of Jesus. All my sins are washed in His blood. God spoke to His people, the Jews, through his prophets and through His own Word, starting with the Garden of Eden and continuing to the coming of Messiah.

It is written: "And I will put enmity between you and the woman, and between your offspring and hers; he will crush your head, and you will strike his heel'" (Gn 3:15 NIV). This came to pass when Jesus' feet were nailed to the cross, and He rose again from the dead and defeated Satan, and the kingdom of darkness came under His feet. God also informed us that Yeshua came from the tribe of Judah out of the twelve tribes of Israel. Today, Jesus is known all over the world as the lion of the tribe of Judah.

It is written: "The scepter will not depart from Judah, nor the ruler's staff from between his feet, until he to whom it belongs shall come and the obedience of the nations shall be his. He will tether his donkey to a vine, his colt to the choicest branch; he will wash his garments in wine, his robes in the blood of grapes" (Gn 49:10-11 NIV). In the book of Zechariah in the bible this prophecy was fulfilled to the letter and in the book of revelation the last and one of the most important book in the bible Jesus returns as a Conqueror to the world and he is riding on a donkey and he is wearing a garment that has been dipped in blood. It is written: "… and his name is the Word of God" (Rv 19:16 NIV). I would also like to point out that Abraham—who is regarded as the father of faith, was the grandfather of Israel, and is revered by Christians, Muslims, and Jews—was visited by the angel of the Lord after passing a very difficult test of obedience from God.

It is written: "The Angel of the LORD called to Abraham from heaven a second time and said, 'By Myself (on the basis of Who I Am) I have sworn [an oath], declares the LORD, that since you have done this thing and have not withheld [from Me] your son, your only son [of promise], indeed I will greatly bless you, and I will greatly multiply your descendants like the stars of the heavens and like the sand on the seashore; and your seed shall possess the gate of their enemies [as conquerors]. Through your seed all the nations of the earth shall be blessed, because you have heard *and* obeyed My voice'" (Gn 22:15-18 AMP).

Israel has become the center of commerce and high tech in the Middle East. God has blessed them immensely. Many Jews who were scattered in Europe and in the North Country (Russia) after their capture by the Assyrian Empire have now returned to their homeland. In Africa, Operation Solomon was a huge success. (The return of Ethiopian Jews back to Israel.) They, too, have a population mix that looks like America. They have one of the best human intelligence agencies in the world, The Mossad. All of the wars Israel has fought since its independence—without going into wars fought 5,000 years ago by Joshua, Moses's heir—were very spectacular and were smashing successes, except the war with Lebanon in 2006, which was to recover twelve Israeli soldiers who were captured by Hezbollah.

At the time when the crisis broke out, I was in Washington D.C. attending the CUFI Conference (Christians United For Israel), lobbying in the capital on behalf of Israel. God informed me that Israel's incursion would be a failure, and even though they started that war with a promise not to involve ground troops, the Holy Spirit told me they would end up sending ground troops and that they would still not recover the twelve soldiers kidnapped by Hezbollah. I was a lonely person then, so when I received this revelation from the Holy Spirit and shared it with my fellow church members, they thought I was out of my mind. But everything God told me would happen did happen. As we were leaving Washington D.C. to return to Minnesota, where I was staying before moving to Texas, CNN announced that Israel was sending troops into Lebanon. To cut the long story short, when Israel did a top to bottom review of that war, they described it as the worst war they had ever fought. There were a lot of missing pieces.

Iran is the place Israel should have attacked, and the soldiers would have been released. This is because the United Nations, the United States, and the whole world were afraid of a wider war. They would have put pressure on Iran, and Iran would have put pressure on Hezbollah. Also, at that time the defense minister in Israel, for the first time in a long time, was not from the tribe of Benjamin. The people of the Benjamin tribe were ordained and anointed

91

from above to hold that position, and then Israel wouldn't lose wars. What was ironic was that Yitzhak Shamir, who was a foreign minister, then acknowledged that Iran was the main player behind the crises but because they did not want a wider regional war, they chose not to attack Iran, which proved to be a failure.

When Pentecost happened, as recorded in the book of Acts, The Holy Spirit appeared in tongues of fire on top of the heads of the 120 people who were gathered together in one place. It came at a time when people from all over the world, including devout Jews, had gathered in Jerusalem to celebrate the Shavuot, which is fifty days after Passover. Today, under the Gregorian calendar, which is the calendar we use in the world, this divine encounter with the Holy Spirit also took place exactly fifty days after Easter. This was done deliberately in order to send a very powerful signal to the Jews (the first fruit of the gospel) that this Holy Spirit was here to continue the work of Jesus, who was the Messiah. Yeshua Himself had promised earlier, before ascending into heaven and sitting down with the Father, that He would send the Holy Spirit to the disciples, all of whom were Jewish.

Moses was the prophet who was most revered by Jews all over the world. You cannot celebrate Passover without remembering how Hashem commissioned Moses to lead His people, the Jews, out of bondage from under their Egyptian task masters, where they were enslaved for over 400 years. God wroth great miracles, signs, and wonders through Moses and the rod that he carried in his right hand.

Moses saw the back of God and basked in His glory twice for forty days. In fact, when he returned from spending time with God on Mount Sinai, the fading glory of God on his face was so bright that he had to cover it because his fellow Jews were frightened to see him. Yet Moses, whom the Bible describes in the Tanakh (Old Testament) as the humblest man, did not make it even to Israel, the promised land that

Jews are now living in. Why is that? All Jews know why. He slapped the rock instead of obeying God, who asked him to speak to the rock just as he was told. That rock was the eternal rock of ages. Just because of this disobedience, he was barred by God from entering into the promised land. Today, you and I can fly to New York from Dallas, catch a flight on EL AL to Tel Aviv, and visit that promised land.

It is written: "And the LORD said to Moses that very same day, 'Go up to this mountain of the Abarim, Mount Nebo, which is in the land of Moab opposite Jericho, and look at the land of Canaan, which I am giving to the sons of Israel as a possession. Then die on the mountain which you climb, and be gathered to your people [in death], just as Aaron your brother died on Mount Hor and was gathered to his people, because you broke faith with Me among of the sons of Israel at waters of Meribah-kadesh, in the Wilderness of Zin, and because you did not treat Me as holy among of the sons of Israel. For you shall see the land opposite you from a distance, but you shall not go there, into the land which I am giving to the children of Israel'" (Dt 32:48-52 AMP).

It was the devil who got Moses to disobey God's instructions by allowing the complaints of the Israelites irritate him, and in his irritation he slapped the rock instead of speaking to it. Yet God loved Moses. He was 120 years old when he died. His eyes were in excellent condition, and he was in top shape, his natural strength not abated. Moses died, and God Himself buried him. Moses was under the law, not under the Abrahamic covenant, which was before the law. Abraham, who is the father of faith, got away with a lot of things, but none of them included disobedience against God. I have good news. Moses did eventually visit the promised land when he appeared with Elijah and met Jesus in the mountain of transfiguration, according to the Holy Scriptures. It is written: "And behold, Moses and Elijah appeared to them, talking with Jesus. Then Peter began to speak and said to Jesus, 'LORD, it is good *and* delightful *and* auspicious that we are here…' While he was still speaking, behold, a bright cloud overshadowed them, and a voice from the cloud said 'This is My beloved Son, with whom I am well-pleased and delighted! Listen to Him'" (Mt 17:3-5 AMP).

There are no revered rabbis on Earth today. No matter how brilliant they are or how many scholastic degrees they may have on Judaism, religion, or the law, they could never be as close to God as Moses was, unless they have received more visitations than Ezekiel, the prophet of God, who was in exile in Babylon. God had set apart Ezekiel because of his obedience, and thus they were protected from death and persecution when they were enslaved by the Babylonians. Think about this for a moment: If Moses, who literally saw the back of God, did not make it to the promised land, which is here on Earth, how are you going to make it to the New Jerusalem? How do you make it to heaven without the blood of the living covenant of Yeshua?

In the book of Isaiah, he prophesied that Jesus would take away our weaknesses, sicknesses, and distresses and that Christ would carry our sorrow and pain. He would be wounded for our transgressions, bruised for our iniquities. The needful obtaining of our peace would come through beatings on his shoulder, and we would be healed.

Without the shedding of blood, there is no remission of sins, and no one knows this more than the Jews. And that blood was shed on the cross of Calvary. The good news is that God has reserved 144,000 Jews who will contend with the antichrist and preach the gospel of Jesus Christ during the end times. Again, Moses was the greatest prophet of God and was revered by the Jews, but Jesus is the greatest Jew who ever lived. The gospel started with the Jews, and it will be completed with them. These 144,000 Jews will have the seal of God on their foreheads. This seal will be of the Holy Spirit, and so when God starts to pour His wrath on the whole Earth, they will be protected and saved from God's wrath. They will be given this protection, just as Ezekiel was, because the Bible says they are virgins and would not have defiled themselves with the sinful things of this world. Hallelujah!

Let Us Pray

Father, in the name of Your Son, Yeshua, I come to You just as I am. I am a sinner before man and, more importantly, before You. I have participated in things that the world considers popular and justified, but You call them sins. Take me as I am and mold me for Your glory. I acknowledge that Yeshua came into this world to die for all my sins—the ones from yesterday, today, and even tomorrow. I understand that this grace pouring out into the world was paid for by the sacrifice of Your only begotten Son on the cross of Calvary. Yeshua the Messiah was fully God and fully man, and His death reconciled me with You. I recognize that a new journey has begun in my life. Send Your Holy Spirit to me and train my heart to live for You. In Yeshua's name I pray. (By saying this prayer, you are reborn. Rejoice, I say. Rejoice!)

Chapter 4

THE BATTLE WITHIN YOU AND A STRATEGY FOR VICTORY

When you are reborn and come to the knowledge of the truth that Jesus is not just your Savior but also the Savior of the entire world, there is great rejoicing in heaven. Yes, the Heavenly Father rejoices. Your name is then written in the Lamb's Books of Life. Christ's spirit of peace will come upon you. You will fill like a weight has been lifted from your shoulders. The fear of death will depart from you immediately because you will know that no one will be able to take your life without God's approval or nod. In a nutshell, your fear will be replaced by a newfound faith in God, and it will grow in strength as you dwell on His Word and obey the Holy Spirit.

It is written: "Since the children have flesh and blood, he too shared in their humanity so that by his death he might break the power of him who holds the power of death—that is the devil—and free those who all their lives were held in slavery by their fear of death" (Heb 2:14-15 NIV).

In addition, from that day, anytime you are in a conversation with anyone on Earth and you say something favorable about God and His Kingdom, the Heavenly Father pays attention to what you said, and it is recorded in heaven. You are immediately delivered from the bondage of darkness through Jesus' blood, even the forgiveness of sins. You are also declared the sons of God. Now, Jesus is the only begotten Son of God, but you become, regardless of gender, what God calls the sons of God, and a powerful position of sonship is bestowed on you. Angels are then dispatched to you. At least two of them are deployed to Earth to watch over you. Some of these angels may already have taken their position around you in order to bring you into salvation. They have a strategic mission, but you are never to worship angels at all, except to ask them to work with you to accomplish heaven's agenda on the earth. Any religion that tells you to worship angels is false, and this is unbiblical. Their assignment is to guide and protect you as you work with the Holy Spirit to enter into those things that are written of you in heaven. Remember again the Lord's Prayer: "...your will be done, on earth as it is in heaven" (Mt 6:10 NIV).

As you begin to read the Bible (God's Word, indeed Jesus in written form), you will become more and more aware of the presence of a very important but invisible person in your life. This person is none other than the Holy Spirit. The Holy Spirit is part of the Trinity. When Jesus was living on the earth, He promised to send the Holy Spirit, who will not be speaking on His own but will be informing you of what Jesus and the Father in heaven are telling you. He will be conveying truth to you, instructing you and guiding you day by day as you begin a new walk in life as God's new creation. This is where the word "reborn" comes from. He will be your advocate on Earth since Jesus is your advocate in heaven. He will be your comforter, your counselor, and the spirit of truth. You will have to learn to always obey His suggestions, though it does take time to discern His voice in your heart. He speaks to the spirit within you. You will have to have quiet time in order to hear what God is saying to you through the Holy Spirit. This is hugely important if you are going to make headway in your new life. Congratulations!

It is written: "And I will ask the Father, and he will give you another advocate to help you and be with you forever—

97

the Spirit of truth. The world cannot accept him, because it neither sees him nor knows him. But you know him, for he lives with you and will be in you" (Jn 14:16-17 NIV).

Know this: In the beginning you will be a baby Christian in need of much spiritual milk. Nevertheless, do not despise small beginnings. Remember, there is absolutely no limit to the deep, personal relationship you can have with God through His Son, Jesus Christ. It is really up to you how far and how fast you want to climb in the realms of the spirit to obtain the promises of God for you. You can choose to have a long-distance relationship with God, staying six feet apart, just like we were instructed to do because of the outbreak of the Coronavirus, or you can accept the fact that you have become a bride of Christ, and therefore you desire intimacy with Him. It is up to you, my brother or sister in Christ. As you grow in the joy and excitement of being reborn, you can tell others if you feel comfortable to do so. God will immediately start using you to speak to others about your decision. Why? As you go about this act of boldness, you will be conferred with another title in heaven. You will be called an Ambassador of Christ. This title literally gives you all the aristocratic and diplomatic rights you are entitled to as a citizen of heaven. No decision can be made on Earth concerning your life without receiving clearance in heaven. Wow! Isn't that something? That's powerful, isn't it? Just as ambassadors from different countries have special protection in the host country, so shall you have an even greater special protection on Earth.

Cooperating with the Holy Spirit will be imperative if you are going to grow and avoid unnecessary spiritual warfare from the kingdom of darkness, who also will be fully aware of your new relationship with God. Just as heaven will be celebrating your decision to be reborn, the kingdom of darkness will be waiting for an opportunity to get you to trip up and to prevent you, if possible, from fulfilling your assignment on Earth. But do not be afraid at all. Never ever

98

give in to fear, for the Bible tells us the presence of the Holy Spirit in you is greater than the devil.

It is written: "You, dear children, are from God and have overcome them, because the one who is in you is greater than the one who is in the world" (1 Jn 4:4 NIV).

The human body is made by God from the dust of the earth. In your body you have your spirit, which God speaks to directly through His Holy Spirit. Your spirit then translates the message to your soul, and then your soul sends it to your body through your mind. You can then make a decision whether to obey or not. The challenge you will face, like all Christians today, is how to subdue your flesh (body) and force it to obey your spirit. Your spirit can never lie or do anything in error. Your spirit is always in right fellowship and agreement with the Holy Spirit, whom I remind you is only relaying God's message to you.

There will always be an attempt by your flesh, where the old you resides, to try to get you to disobey God. So, the old you and your born-again spirit will be at odds for a long time, until you allow one to emerge victorious over the other. Joyce Meyers, one of the great evangelist of our generation, calls it the battlefield of the mind, and she wrote a book about it. Indeed, Joyce has written several books about this topic. She is a prolific speaker, and her teachings on this subject are truly anointed of God. I strongly urge you to invest a few dollars in getting one of them, and invest in her ministry. It would do you much good in winning the battle within and advancing your loving relationship with God.

Listen, my dear friend, and hear me loud and clear. The flesh profits nothing. In the flesh dwells pride, anger, bitterness, unforgiveness, impatience, lying, selfishness, greed, hatred, jealousy, lust, fault finding, murder, and the one who facilitated the killing of many people during the Coronavirus pandemic: the evil spirit of fear. Fear comes from Satan, just as faith comes from God. All of these things were in you when Jesus, through the Holy Spirit, drew you to Him. Isn't He lovely? I remember hearing "Isn't She Lovely?" by Steven Wonder. God is awesome, just awesome!

In the secular world, and even among Christian ministries, people are hired for work based on their credentials and their ability to show through the interview process that they can do the job. With God it is different. He takes you in your broken and fallen state, accepts you as you are, and molds you into a new creation. All of those character flaws are taken away from you, one by one, as you work with Him. He does this because He absorbed all of your sins and flaws in the body of Christ on the cross of Calvary, and therefore in His eyes you are spotless. God brought Jesus to fulfill the law we couldn't keep. You must always remember this truth, or Satan will work through your mind to condemn you and accuse you through others anytime you fall short of living like a child of God. Always respond with the Word. If God be for me, who can be against me? I am redeemed from the curse of the law. My sins have been washed by the blood of the Lamb. Nevertheless, do not abuse this freedom God has given you to enter into His Kingdom through His Son, Jesus Christ.

It is written: "Christ purchased our freedom *and* redeemed us from the curse of the Law *and* its condemnation by becoming a curse for us—for it is written, 'CURSED IS EVERYONE WHO HANGS [crucified] ON A TREE (cross)'— in order that in Christ Jesus the blessing of Abraham might also come to the Gentiles, so that we would all receive [the realization of] the promise of the [Holy] Spirit through faith" (Gal 3:13-14 AMP).

This is true love personified, a love that the whole world today yearns for but is unable to obtain. The sacrificial love of God through His Son is available to all who ask for it. The world may not know it, but the reason the world has become chaotic is because true peace that surpasses all human understanding is found in Christ Jesus alone. Jesus

Christ said this while he walked the earth more than 2,000 years ago.

It is written: "Peace I leave with you; My [perfect] peace I give to you; not as the world gives do I give to you. Do not let your heart be troubled, nor let it be afraid. [Let My perfect peace calm you in every circumstance and give you courage and strength for every challenge.]" (Jn 14:27 AMP).

This is why Jesus said on a historic visit to Jerusalem more than 2,000 years ago that Israel would not see the peace she is looking for until His return, when they would say with their own mouths, "Blessed be he that cometh in the name of the LORD..." (Ps 118:26 KJV). Even these very words about what Jesus said were sang prophetically by King David in a thanksgiving service to God about 1,000 years before Jesus arrived in Jerusalem. And then Jesus Himself added another prophecy on top of the fulfillment of David's prophetic song.

It is written: "For I say to you, you will not see Me again [ministering to you publicly] until you say, 'BLESSED [to be celebrated with praise] IS HE WHO COMES IN THE NAME OF THE LORD!'" (Mt 23:39 AMP).

Since then, every effort to bring lasting peace to that region—an effort made by some of the greatest statesmen, U.S. presidents, and skilled negotiators with the best diplomatic credentials—has been an exercise in futility. It has come to nothing. That is, apart from the Camp David Accord, which brokered a peace treaty between Egypt and Israel to avoid a wider Middle East war. We know, according to Bible prophecy, that the antichrist will establish a temporary peace between the Palestinian leaders and the government of Israel, but it will begin to fall apart after forty-two months and will bring about the slaughter of innocent Jews in East Jerusalem. So grotesque it will be when they literally slash pregnant Jewish women's unborn babies from their wombs. This crisis will then culminate in the triumphant return of the Messiah before they overrun

Israel completely, and Jesus Himself will establish lasting peace on the entire earth.

You see, Jesus is known as the Prince of peace. True peace, without any strings attached, is found in Him and Him alone. Jesus' peace always brings calm to you personally. It is a reassuring peace that will allow everything to be well with your soul. It takes worrying out of the picture. It comes to reassure you of His loving kindness so you can get through the temporary problems you are facing. Above all, it is a reward from Hashem, our Father in heaven, for trusting in His Son.

It is written: "You will keep in perfect *and* constant peace *the one* whose mind is steadfast [that is, committed and focused on You—in both inclination and character], Because he trusts *and* takes refuge in You [with hope and confident expectation]" (Is 26:3 AMP).

So one of the things you will want to quickly develop within yourself is the ability to cast your burdens on the good Lord, because He cares for you affectionately. You will find purpose in your heart as you grow in the knowledge of the things of God by dwelling and meditating on His Word in the free time you have. Seek His advice before talking to other wise people about any problems you encounter. This will teach you how to begin to hear the Lord speaking to you in your heart. Jesus always has your best interests at heart, and He comes with no ulterior motives or hidden agendas. This is because it was Jesus, and no one else, who purchased your freedom from the kingdom of darkness by laying down His life for you.

It is written: "Greater love hath no man than this, that a man lay down his life for his friends" (Jn 15:13 KJV). Jesus was the sacrificial Lamb that reconciled with God after the Fall of Adam, and our sins were placed on Jesus. This is something you must always have in your heart if you are to remain steadfast in the things of God while you are on this earth. There will be all kinds of diverse temptations trying to pull you back at every opportunity. Embrace the light of Christ and shut yourself off from the things of the world that will hinder your walk with God. Allow Christ's light to shine on you ever so brightly as things on Earth get increasingly dark and the land becomes full of iniquity. Isaiah, the prophet, saw what our generation would be witnessing and spoke nearly 3,000 years ago about the assuring hope of Christ's light shining on us even in the midst of the darkness.

It is written: "'Arise, shine, for your light has come, and the glory of the LORD rises upon you. See, darkness covers the earth and thick darkness is over the peoples, but the LORD rise upon you and his glory appears over you" (Is 60:1-2 NIV).

One is not asking you to isolate yourself from the people of this world, for this would not be wisdom and would be next to impossible. What I am encouraging you to do is influence the world for good. Encourage your friends, colleagues, families, and associates to come to the knowledge of Christ rather than you being influenced by them to keep doing things that are disobedient in the eyes of God.

God is love, and He loves you. Feel His presence as He wraps Himself around you. Always keep the truth that God loves you dearly, like you are His only child in the world, in the front, center, and back of your mind. It doesn't matter what people think about you as long as your ways are pleasing to the Lord. In fact, if you endeavor to please the Lord in all you do, God will protect you from your enemies, both physical and spiritual. It is written: "When the LORD takes pleasure in anyone's way, he causes their enemies to make peace with them" (Prv 16:7 NIV).

The book of Proverbs was written to a large extent by King Solomon, who was regarded as the wisest ruler in his time. The book provides wise practical applications on how to live your life on Earth and address real-life situations. They involve a lot of wise sayings that can be applied to one's daily routine. The important thing to note is that there are thirty-one proverbs in the bible. One for each day of the month. It will do you much good to read, and indeed ponder, one proverb a day. What will happen, as you learn some of these proverbs by heart, when the spirit of wisdom, which is one of the seven spirits of God, comes upon you. In a matter of time, you will begin to stand out among your peers, and the world will begin to take notice. You will not be easily deceived. You will begin to master how to approach every situation you face with tact, wisdom, and understanding. This will come the more you dwell on the Word of God and give priority to the Word of God over the things of this world. Every problem you face will become an opportunity to glorify God in the solutions that will be given to you by the Holy Spirit. The Holy Spirit will become more active in your life.

The Bible is an explosively powerful book that will become your sword (a spiritual weapon) the moment you become reborn. When you are reborn, you want to start reading the book of Genesis in the Old Testament at the same time you read the gospel in the New Testament: Matthew, Mark, Luke, and John. The book of Genesis will demonstrate the awesome power of God from the beginning of creation right up to Joseph, who was humbled to become a Christ-like figure and eventually became the vice president of Egypt even though he was a Hebrew boy from Israel. At that time Egypt was the superpower of the whole world. You will learn how Joseph went from the prison to the palace under unusual circumstances because he had found favor with God. Joseph, the Hebrew son of Jacob, was sold by his jealous brothers as a slave to Egyptian slave traders. He was then sold by the Ishmaelite slave traders to a high-ranking official of the Egyptian government, who was head of the security detail (brigade of guards) of the pharaoh (Royal King of Egypt) 5,000 years ago. The head of the brigade of guards for the pharaoh was Potiphar. In other words, if you

104

wanted to attack or assassinate the pharaoh, you had to go through this man and his heavily trained, seasoned men of war. He was the captain of the guard.

It is written: "The LORD was with Joseph so that he prospered, and he lived in the house of his Egyptian master. When his master saw that the LORD was with him and that the LORD gave him success in everything he did, Joseph found favor in his eyes and became his attendant. Potiphar put him in charge of his household, and he entrusted to his care everything he owned. From the time he put him in charge of his household and of all that he owned, the LORD blessed the household of the Egyptian because of Joseph. The blessing of the LORD was on everything Potiphar had, both in the house and in the field. So Potiphar left everything he had in Joseph's care; with Joseph in charge, he did not concern himself with anything excerpt the food he ate" (Gn 39:2-7 NIV).

Today, there are Broadway plays throughout the world depicting the life of Joseph and what he went through as one of the sons of Jacob before God vindicated him and glorified His name in Joseph's life. If you are unfamiliar with this story, read chapters thirty-seven through fifty of Genesis. Unfortunately, there is one problem with the Broadway musical called *Joseph And His Amazing Technicolor*, and the problem is that the people who wrote this play go to great lengths not to allow its audience to recognize it is based on the biblical story of Joseph. They mask the fact that it is based on true story. They do not reference God in any way. Powerful leaders in Washington and Europe are going out of their way to discredit the Bible, not knowing that they are provoking the wrath of God upon their nations.

The best way to continue to grow in the knowledge of the things of God, and to fight the temptation of going back to your old way of life, is to surround yourself with godly, reborn people. Join a church that delights in the study of the Word of God. Temptations will come, but you will

105

overcome them with the help of God. When temptations come, it is either because of the sin nature within you or because of the devil himself, who knows what is ahead of you. The devil sometimes tempts us when a promotion from God is coming. Satan seeks to delay or outrightly deny the children of God their due blessings from God by getting them to fall for his bait. God allows it because He does not want to elevate you to a high position only for you to fall disgracefully because you hadn't developed the character and discipline needed to endure the trials that might come with that promotion.

It is written: "When tempted, no one should say, 'God is tempting me.' For God cannot be tempted by evil, nor does he tempt anyone; but each person is tempted when they are dragged away by their own evil desire and enticed" (Jas 1:13-14 NIV).

Joseph was tempted before he became vice president of a foreign country he was not even born in. And even though, by God's grace, he did not yield to the temptation, he did not immediately get promoted. He had to go to prison because he was wrongly accused of falling for the temptation when, in reality, he did not. Eventually, God rescued him and elevated him through unusual circumstances, which demonstrated, once again, the majestic, awesome, omniscient, and great power of God, who rules and reigns over all the affairs of men. God is great.

But when you fall into temptation, it does not in any way take away your salvation. Shake it off by repenting (turning away from that sin or signaling to God your desire to turn away from that lifestyle), and God will cleanse you.

Do not allow condemnation and guilt from Satan take root in your heart. They are not from God. Your Heavenly Father prefers for you to move on and forget about it after asking for forgiveness. More than anything else, keep reminding yourself that you are the righteousness of God in Christ Jesus.

Keep saying to yourself daily: Christ has redeemed me from the curse of the law. The more you openly declare who you are in Christ Jesus, the more you become what you declare, and Satan can't easily trip you up. Your carnal mindset (natural mindset) will make you feel that you are very bad and evil because of what you are thinking. I have been there, and every Christian, without exception, has been there. Don't be dismayed one bit. Shake it off rather than dwell on it. I tell you that these are invisible arrows of suggestion that come from the old man within you, long influenced by Satan. Don't accept it as coming from you. You have to learn to cast those ideas down and replace them with the Word of God, which affirms and confirms who you are in Christ Jesus.

It is written: "For though we walk in the flesh [as mortal men], we are not carrying on our [spiritual] warfare according to the flesh *and* using the weapons of man. The weapons of our warfare are not physical [weapons of flesh and blood]. Our weapons are divinely powerful for the destruction of fortresses. *We are* destroying sophisticated arguments and every exalted *and* proud thing that sets itself up against the [true] knowledge of God, and *we are* taking every thought *and* purpose captive to the obedience of Christ" (2 Cor 10:3-5 AMP).

Always try to have a positive mindset. Do not dwell on everything that comes to your mind.

Instead, filter it through the Word of God. From time to time, as you go about your daily routine, ask yourself, "Does this thought glorify God," anytime something comes into your mind that you know you shouldn't be entertaining or dwelling on. It takes time, and it isn't going to be easy, but keep in mind that the human brain processes about thiry-four GB a day according to a study done by Roger Bon at the University of California in San Diego. That is a sufficient enough amount of information to overwhelm a laptop within a week. Your mind will have to be renewed from you old way of life. With time you will eventually begin to enjoy the benefits of having the mind of Christ. You will experience freedom and total victory as you master this human ability to manage thought processes. Paul of Tarsus was an apostle of Christ, and he wrote the book of Philippians in the Bible. He gave some pretty good advice to Christians.

It is written: "Finally, believers, whatever is true and whatever is honorable *and* worthy of respect, whatever is right *and* confirmed by God's word, whatever is pure *and* wholesome, whatever is lovely *and* brings peace, whatever is admirable *and* of good repute; if there is any excellence, if there is anything worthy of praise, think *continually* on these things [center your mind on them, and implant them in your heart]. The things which you have learned and received and heard and seen in me, practice these things [in daily life], and the God [who is the source] of peace *and* well-being will be with you" (Phil 4:8-10 AMP).

Yes, I am telling you to let go of your old mind and put on the new mind of Christ. You will do well, through constant meditation on the Word of God, to avoid the sins I mentioned in Chapter 2, such as swearing. In most cases, once you become reborn, your desire to curse almost automatically goes away because it just wouldn't feel right coming out of your mouth anymore. This was my experience. You will also begin to enjoy and be proud of yourself for being able to speak in clear sentences without having to use the F-word and the S-word. In the past you felt cool doing it, but now your renewed mind has empowered you to please God with what you do with your body. Of course, there will be slipups, but don't let that make you think you haven't graduated from your past life. Repent and move on. You will become very sensitive to others using foul language when they speak, but do not be judgmental. Rather than rebuking them, use this as an opportunity to minister the gospel of Christ to them. Once they get free, they, too, will figure it out. Anytime you hear someone curse, remember

108

that this was where you were before Christ drew you by His grace to Himself. Do not become the taskmaster shooting down anyone who uses a curse word, except in your own household. Did you know that you do not own your own body? It also does not belong to your parents. Who owns you? You will be surprised what the Bible says, but this is hugely important as you begin your new life walking with God.

It is written: "What? know ye not that your body is the temple of the Holy Ghost which is in you, which ye have of God, and ye are not your own? For ye are bought with a price: therefore glorify God in your body, and in your spirit, which are God's" (1 Cor 6:19-20 KJV).

As we can all observe based on what is written in the Bible, we have a landlord. We are tenants, and we can't just allow anything into our bodies, nor can we use them for things God frowns upon, regardless of whether it is popular. All of these things are temporary, and they will pass away, but the Word of God will stand forever. Let me explain this abovementioned biblical verse in a way that rings true to the heart. Imagine you own a block of apartments. You will certainly have a say as to who can rent from you. Each person wanting to live in your apartment will fill out an application. They will agree not to grow weed or allow it to be run over by rodents. There will be an initial damage or security deposit. Sometimes you will ask for first payment before they even get the keys. You won't rent to people who have been evicted several times for violating one apartment rule after another.

It is the same with God, who wants you to be very fruitful with your life on Earth. If you think about it carefully for a moment, many people have tried to come into the world but unfortunately did not make it. Maybe they died because they were stillborn upon delivery. Maybe they were miscarried or aborted, or maybe they died of sudden infant death syndrome. Or maybe they died from malaria in the less developed nations of the world, where hunger and malaria are prevalent. However, by divine providence, you got to make it, and you now have an opportunity to fulfill your destiny. It is only fair that God demands some form of accountability from you in how you take care of yourself while on Earth. Do not allow anything to enslave you, whether it is food addiction, sugar addiction, drug addiction, anger, or other devices in the world. Christ died to set you free, and whom the Lord sets free is free indeed.

The Bible is full of the expressed love of God for all people who are called by His name. He never judges us according to our sins. He is slow to anger and plenteous in mercy. He makes allowances for people, hoping that not one person should perish (eternal damnation) but that they would all come to the knowledge of the truth. He has compassion on all He has made. He opens His hand and satisfies the desires of every living thing. He is well acquainted with our shortcomings and our fears. King David said this about God more than 3,000 years ago: "...thy loving kindness is better than life..." (Ps 63:3 KJV). David, the giant killer, wasn't perfect. He was far from perfect. He lived under the old covenant, unlike you and me. So, when he sinned, he was punished because he was under the Mosaic law, and the foundation was the ten commandments and the 635 Levitical laws. Yet his love and praises for God can be found throughout the Bible, especially in the book of Psalms. As for you and me, we are under the grace covenant, in which the foundation is the sacrificial crucifixion of Jesus Christ for all our sins. This, more than anything else, should embolden us to live lives worthy of our calling and, above all, lives that are an expression of who we belong to, which is the Almighty God.

It is written: "Let your light so shine before men, that they may see your good works, and glorify your Father which is in heaven" (Mt 5:16 KJV).

Finally, as children of God, our Heavenly Father wants us to pursue our work with our various employers like we would if we were working for Him. He wants us to be diligent in our work, examples of excellent workers who are steadfast in keeping commitments and exceeding client expectations. God says that we belong to Him, and He wants all His children to be role models for the people of this world. He doesn't want our individual ministry to be discredited because we are slothful and are bad examples to our colleagues and employers. If, on the other hand, we are at the top in terms of recognition and performance, it reflects a great deal on our individual ministry and on the God we serve. It is easier to minister the gospel to your colleagues if you are always doing well and outperforming your peers. Never forget to ask for God's grace as you replace your old lifestyle with a lifestyle that glorifies God. We are told in the book of Hebrew to come boldly to the throne of grace and find mercy in times of need. God's grace is sufficient enough to empower you to live your life for Christ, even when you are down and out.

Let Us Pray

I pray that out of His glorious riches He will strengthen you with power through His spirit, so that Christ may dwell in your hearts through faith. And I pray that you, being rooted and established in love, may have power, together with all the Lord's holy people, to grasp how wide and how long and how high and how deep the love of Christ is, and to know this love that surpasses knowledge can fill you up. Now, to Him who is able to do immeasurably more than all we ask or imagine, according to His power that is at work within us, we give glory to You and Christ Jesus throughout all generations, forever and ever! May the grace of our Lord Jesus Christ and the sweet fellowship of His Holy Spirit be with us now and forevermore. Amen.

111

Chapter 5

JESUS IS THE TRUE VINE. HE LITERALLY TELLS YOU WHAT TO DO

This is one of my favorite chapters because it embodies how much God loves us dearly. This chapter lets you know that God treasures you and desires deep fellowship with you throughout your lifetime here on Earth.

So, my question to you is this: How would you like to take an exam where all the answers are provided for you or, at the very least, clues are set in place to make it easy for you to grasp the correct answers? The answer to this question from most people would be, "It sounds like cheating, but I will take it." Yes, it would seem unfair to those who do not have the answers. However, what if the answers were made available to everybody who would partake in this exam? The only requirement is that you believe the answers you obtain are the right answers. I am using an analogy that pales in comparison to the real topic, which is the reward of heaven, which you can only receive if you believe in the answer: Jesus.

It is written: "I am the vine, ye are the branches: He that abideth in me, and I in him, the same bringeth forth much fruit: for without me ye can do nothing" (Jn 15:5 KJV).

If you are not familiar with the King James Version, the Amplified Bible makes it clearer.

It is written: "I am the Vine; you are the branches. The one who remains in Me and I in him bears much fruit, for [otherwise] apart from Me [that is, cut off from vital union with Me] you can do nothing" (Jn 15:5 AMP).

Everything seems to pertain to fruit in some way. It just dawned on me that we live in a fallen world because Adam and Eve ate fruit from the wrong tree. So now, in order to not repeat the same mistakes and flunk the eternity exam, Jesus is telling us in the Word of God that we should partake of the good fruit from the good tree. The vine from that tree is Jesus Himself. He is telling you and me that we cannot make it or discover our true purpose in life without Him. He is telling us that we must stay close to Him if we are going to make any headway in living life abundantly, which He desires for all mankind. Jesus is clearly underscoring a solemn truth that He is the answer, the gateway to eternity, and the bearing of fruit on earth that is worthy and acceptable in heaven. Jesus is saying, "Oh yes, there are other trees, and there are other fruits, but if you want to receive your reward when you depart from this earth, you are going to need to hang around with Me." Indeed, you are going to need to draw nourishment from Him. You need to allow him to carry you step by step so God can glorify His name in your life's work. You will be working hand in hand with the Holy Spirit. That said, you must come to the solemn realization that "…it is by grace you have been saved, through faith—and this is not from yourselves, it is the gift of God—not by works, so that no can boast" (Eph 2:8-9 NIV). Jesus put grace in place, and grace we have received.

Everybody is born into this world for a particular purpose, usually to solve a unique problem. Everyone who has a successful run in life always encounters a divine helper who propels him to a level of greatness he would not have obtained without the helper. Jesus was fully God and fully man when He came upon the earth. Yet He used twelve disciples, with Paul of Tarsus replacing Judas after he betrayed Him, to spread the gospel to all parts of the earth. Before He started His ministry, He asked John the Baptist to baptize Him. John, knowing who Jesus was, was very reluctant to do it, but Jesus told him to go ahead. John felt it should be the other way around, with Jesus baptizing him.

But Jesus was showing us that we need each other to accomplish more for the Kingdom of God collectively. In summary, Jesus is the only way to make it to heaven and, above all, the only way to achieve something tangible within your life that carries weight in heaven. There are many people all over the world who do not know Jesus and have gone on to do great things on the earth. The main question is this: Did their work on Earth become sweet-smelling in the eyes of God?

It is written: "For what does it benefit a man to gain the whole world [with all its pleasures], and forfeit his soul?" (Mk 8:36 AMP)

If you are a multimillionaire but a drug dealer, how does this glorify God? If you are a Wall Street baron and a billionaire but you never helped to spread the gospel, let alone advance the Kingdom of God, how does your work measure up in heaven? Seeking the Kingdom of God and His righteousness is not only the right way to pursue your earthly goals; it is also good for your life in heaven. Jesus is the answer to all of the problems you will encounter in life, and He is your burden bearer. He would never take advantage of you; He will always lead you on the right path.

It is written in the Bible: "'Call to Me and I will answer you, and tell you [and even show you] great and mighty things, [things which have been confined and hidden], which you do not know *and* understand *and* cannot distinguish'" (Jer 33:3 AMP). Jesus, through the Holy Spirit, wants to spare all of us from living arduous and tiresome lives, trying to figure out what exactly we are called to do. The various bunny trails we take in life often lead to unfulfillment. This happens even when you are rich and have houses and

114

condos all over the world. True happiness is found in Christ, the solid rock. It isn't necessary to depend on the abundance of your possessions. Many wealthy people constantly deal with the headache of other people wanting to either defraud them or take advantage of them.

It is written: "If anyone does not remain in Me, he is thrown out like a [broken off] branch, and withers *and* dies; and they gather such branches and throw them into the fire, and they are burned. If you remain in Me and My words remain in you [that is, if we are vitally united and My message lies in your heart], ask whatever you wish and it will be done for you. My Father is glorified *and* honored by this, when you bear much fruit, and prove yourselves to be My [true] disciples" (Jn 15:6-8 AMP).

God wants us to come to Him so He can save us time and help us avoid the frustrations in life that many go through. This is true for the reborn and those who are not. In life every one of us will eventually come to a fork in the road. One, then, must decide which way to go. One way will lead you to your God-given potential, and the other road will take you far from it. To enter into the Kingdom of God on Earth, you must discover your purpose. The Kingdom of God is not about eating and drinking; it's about peace, love, and joy in the Holy Ghost. If you are on a journey full of ups and downs and no real fruit, turn around, go on bended knees, and seek the face of the Father earnestly, so that He may lead you along the right path while you are on the earth. Do not be misled or deceived by other people who just want to take advantage of you.

It is written: "By their fruit you will recognize them [that is, by their contrived doctrine and selffocus]. Do people pick grapes from thorn bushes or figs from thistles? Even so, every healthy tree bears good fruit, but the unhealthy tree bears bad fruit. A good tree cannot bear bad fruit, nor can a bad tree bear good fruit. Every tree that does not bear good fruit is cut down and thrown into the fire. Therefore, by their fruit you will recognize them [as false prophets]" (Mt 7:16-20 AMP).

So, in this era of the internet and social media, it is important you follow Jesus and not some imposter posing to be a follower of Christ. There will be many false prophets; Jesus warned us of this. If you spend time with the Word of God and allow the Holy Spirit to give you understanding, you will not be easily deceived, nor will you follow the wrong path or the wrong person.

Sometimes the pressures of life and a lack of faith keep many people, including Christians, from fulfilling their calling. There are literally billions of people in jobs they were never called to do, even though they got through the necessary training and education to obtain those jobs. Many took the jobs because they paid well or offered tenure. As the world turns, many are finding themselves in stressful situations, and this has begun to affect their health and wellbeing. Discovering your true purpose in life is the ultimate joy. It involves a key component—apart from anchoring your soul with Jesus—and that is that you must have faith. The Bible tells us to be very careful how we live our lives. We should be wise and make the most of every opportunity, as the days are evil. It goes on to tell us not to be foolish but to understand what the Lord's will is for our lives.

On the other hand, there are some people who have had God reveal to them what they are supposed to do through dreams, the prophetic Word, or the Holy Spirit. The Holy Spirit may not have revealed everything, but they have enough information to get going on the assignment. However, they are still wasting time. Since you cannot see your future unless it is revealed in its entirety to you through dreams by God Himself, you must take a leap of faith to enter into the things that are written of you in heaven. The challenge that keeps people from fulfilling their destiny is fear. They may not have the resources, tools, or people they need in order to walk into their destiny. This God's way of testing their allegiance to Him, seeing whether they can trust Him enough to move forward by faith, for the just shall live by faith. Now, there are rare, extraordinary exceptions, such as when someone knows for certain what he was called to do immediately when he arrives on the earth. This takes us to the story of Jesus and His cousin John the Baptist. When John was in his mother's womb, he was aware of his assignment. And he leapt with joy in his mother's womb the moment he heard that Mary, the mother of Jesus, was pregnant with Jesus. John's assignment was to bring Israel to repentance and to prepare the way for the coming of the Messiah. Isaiah, the first writing prophet of Israel, had spoken about John the Baptist around 700 years before he was born. He was exactly as Isaiah described him when he came to the earth.

It is written: "And he went into all the country around the Jordan, preaching a baptism of repentance for the forgiveness of sin; as it is written *and* forever remains written in the book of the words of Isaiah the prophet..." (Lk 3:3-4 AMP).

Amazingly, John said some things that were strikingly like the message of Jesus. He, too, talked about fruit.

It is written: "So he *began* saying to the crowds who were coming out to be baptized by him, 'You brood of vipers, who warned you to flee from the wrath [of God that is] to come? Therefore produce fruit that is worthy of [and consistent with your] repentance [that is, live changed lives, turn from sin and seek God and His righteousness]" (Lk 3:7-8 AMP).

When you have a divine encounter, you can discover your purpose through God's grace. However, there are certain criteria that God expects the reborn to meet. They must have a spirit of repentance and turn away from their sins, especially the sin of unforgiveness and the sins He has been asking them to do away with. Now, no one is

117

perfect; we all have a sinful nature as descendants of Adam. But remember that we are new creations in Christ Jesus. Therefore, Jesus died on the cross to cleanse us from all our sins. In that sacrifice by Jesus, we were given the power to live right. In addition, it gave us access to everything that pertains to godliness and good living, as recorded in the Bible in 1 Peter and 2 Peter. It is written: "For His divine power has bestowed on us [absolutely] everything necessary for [a dynamic spiritual] life and godliness, through true *and* personal knowledge of Him who called us by His own glory and excellence. For by these He has bestowed on us His precious and magnificent promises [of inexpressible value], so that by them you may escape from the immoral freedom that is in the world because of disreputable desire, and become sharers of the divine nature" (2 Pt 1:3-4 AMP).

It is written: "Blessed [gratefully praised and adored] be the God and Father of our Lord Jesus Christ, who according to His abundant *and* boundless mercy has caused us to born again [that is, to be reborn from above—spiritually transformed, renewed, and set apart for His purpose] to an ever-living hope *and* confident assurance through the resurrection of Jesus Christ from the dead..." (1 Pt 1:3 AMP).

God expects us not to insatiably practice a life of sin. Yet God understands that the world we live in today can make it easier to get ensnared in bad habits if we do not keep the eyes of our hearts focused on Jesus Christ.

It is written: "So submit to [the authority of] God. Resist the devil [stand firm against him] and he will flee from you. Come close to God [with a contrite heart] and He will come close to you" (Jas 4:7-8 AMP).

God wants us to move forward in the pursuit of our destiny, even in our imperfect state. But keep in mind that your sin can expose you and shortchange your destiny if not subdued. You do not want to be put in an embarrassing situation. Read the story of Samson in the book of Judges. The truth is, you must hate your sin enough to have a will to turn away from it while, at the same time, crying out to God Almighty for deliverance. It is good to have intercessors who will lift you up in prayer. Talk about your problems with close confidants so they aren't used against you by the enemy, preventing you from fulfilling your God-given destiny. God wants to deliver His people because Christ has already paid for the deliverance on the cross of Calvary. May God Almighty, whose mercies endureth forever, help you in your effort to overcome whatever besets you. In Jesus' name. Amen.

It is written: "But upon mount Zion shall be deliverance, and there shall be holiness; and the house of Jacob shall possess their possessions" (Ob 1:17 KJV). Secondly, do not have unforgiveness toward anyone. As the Bible says, "… let not the sun go down upon your wrath" (Eph 4:26 KJV). If you can't shake off a pain or hurt from someone, here is an old trick: start praying for them and pleading their case before God. Instantly, that spirit of unforgiveness will depart from you. Thirdly, obey whatever God tells you, even if you are afraid to move forward. Never let fear deter you from fulfilling your calling in life. It is from Satan, and he comes to steal your destiny.

On numerous occasions Jesus said that those who love Him obey His commandments. Obedience is important. God cannot work with a person who simply cannot obey simple instructions. Fourthly, walk in love. This, more than anything else, will define your ministry by allowing you to share God's love to people who need to feel that love. Love covers a multitude of sins. Become a vessel through which God's love can flow to the outside world, so that more will come to Christ and be saved.

Finally, follow what was written in Psalm 1 by King David, who was writing this Psalm about his life experience. Remember, David was described by God as a man after God's own heart. God loved David. In a nutshell, meditate daily on the Word of God. This will build your spirit, allow you to walk in obedience, and help you overcome diverse temptations that will come upon this generation.

It is written: "Blessed [fortunate, prosperous, and favored by God] is the man who does not walk in the counsel of the wicked [following their advice and example], Nor stand in the path of sinners, Nor sit [down to rest] in the seat of scoffers (ridiculers). But his delight is in the law of the LORD, And on His law [His precepts and teachings] he [habitually] mediates day and night. And he will be like a tree *firmly* planted [and fed] by streams of water, Which yields its fruit in its season; Is leaf does not wither; And in whatever he does, he prospers [and comes to maturity]. The wicked [those who live in disobedience to God's law] are not so… Therefore the wicked will not stand [unpunished] in the judgement, Nor sinners in the assembly of the righteous" (Ps 1:1-5 AMP).

Let Us Pray

Sovereign Lord, Adonai, who can be compared to You? You are far more awesome than those who surround Your throne. The highest angelic beings stand in awe of You. You are majestic in holiness, awesome in praises, and a worker of miracles. You are the author and finisher of our faith. We thank you for giving us the opportunity to seek Your face 24/7. We are indeed a privileged generation of believers. We ask, and we shall receive. We seek, and we shall find. We knock, and the door will be opened for us. Therefore, we come before Your presence asking You to lead us in the right direction. Be the lamp unto our feet and a light unto our path. Through Your Son, Jesus Christ, we hope to bear much fruit so that Your name may be glorified in our lives. Since we sitteth in the heavenly realms with You, we deploy, with Your permission from on high, the mighty power of Christ's resurrection—the power that was deployed to raise Him in triumphant victory from the dead— against all physical and spiritual opposition in order to fulfill our God-given destiny. We give You praise and glory for opening our eyes and allowing us to know what our purpose is. In Jesus' name we pray. Amen.

Chapter 6

THE WRATH OF GOD AND THE GREAT AWAKENING

It is written: "For the grace of God has appeared that offers salvation to all people. It teaches us to say "No" to ungodliness and worldly passions, and to live self-controlled, upright and godly lives in this present age, while we wait for the blessed hope—the appearing of the glory of our great God and Savior, Jesus Christ, who gave himself for us to redeem us from all wickedness and to purify for himself a people that are his very own, eager to do what is good" (Ti 2:11-14 NIV).

God wants to speak to this generation about things to come. God is interested in revealing to us, particularly the youth and young adults, certain things that He believes will do us much good if we will only listen. God is aware of what is unfolding in the world today, particularly in America and Western Europe. Many young adults are disconnected with the things of God. Yet there are still some whose hearts stay on God because they trust in Him, and they are enjoying the peace that comes with that trust, although many have undergone diverse trials. Unfortunately, they are also noticed by the kingdom of darkness and Satan. He thus works arduously to frustrate these devoted ones, attempting to wear them out. Yet their closeness to God gives them power to resist the devil, and he flees from them.

We are at the peripheral of what is known as the end times, and so more wickedness, chaos, anarchy, and rebellion against divine authority will pervade the earth. It is more difficult than ever to raise a kid in this world today. Parents struggle each day on how best to protect their children from all the vices on the earth without restricting their freedom to live a life of abundance, as Jesus desires for all mankind. The Bible spoke clearly of these times and was very specific in explaining to the world what is unfolding before our eyes. Evil appears to fill the earth, and we hear of one crime after the other—crimes that defy conventional wisdom and make us question whether we are actually better than the animals in the wild. The heart of man today seems constantly obsessed with evil. Even the most pious of us have thoughts we would be embarrassed for others to know about. Most of these thought come from the sin nature within us as well as from the invisible suggestions from the kingdom of darkness. Every one of us, like it or not, carries a seed of the tree of the knowledge of good and evil that was in the Garden of Eden.

In the past we used science to find cures for diseases. Today, we are using science to enlarge the size of our fowls; to modify the crops we grow, altering our food chain forever; and to produce certain growth hormones for our bodies. In most cases, many of these changes have some tangible health benefits, and in certain cases, they can amount to the creation of superhuman beings. There is a fine line, and we have to be careful. We are dangerously breaching the gap between using science for good purposes and altering the human gene for diabolic purposes. With so much information available in this era, as was predicted accurately in the Bible by Daniel in chapter twelve of his book, we humans have begun to enter into uncharted waters that, if we are not careful, could end up doing us more harm than good. Just before God destroyed the world with water during the time of Noah, he talked about His regret in creating human beings, and this indeed was very sad.

It is written: "The LORD saw how great the wickedness of the human race had become on the earth, and that every inclination of the thoughts of the human heart was only evil all the time. The LORD regretted that he had made human beings on the earth, and his heart was deeply troubled.

... But Noah found favor in the eyes of the LORD" (Gn 6:5-8 NIV).

Let me remind the whole world again: God has sworn to once again shake the earth and roll up the heavens. What is unfortunate is that the things God despises are now prevalent in the advanced nations of the world, particularly the western nations. Therefore, no nation is immune from the sins that God hates. The United States and the western nations have always been known, right up to the middle of the 20th century, for spreading the gospel all over the world. And God blessed America, giving her both economic and military clout in order to win the Cold War, and we haven't had another global war since World War II. While Americans, and people from other western nations, have continued to praise the Lord, they have also allowed the things of Satan to flow out of them to every part of the world, contaminating the whole earth, and God is not happy, to say the least. Know this today, brethren: A faucet cannot pour hot and cold water at the same time. You can manipulate it, but the most you will get is lukewarm water. And we know what God has to say about lukewarm water.

It is written: "These are the words of the Amen, the faithful and true witness, the ruler of God's creation. I know your deeds, that you are neither cold nor hot. I wish you were either one or the other!

So, because you are lukewarm—neither hot nor cold—I am about to spit you out of my mouth" (Rv 3:14-16 NIV).

God is saying that if you are hot (on fire for Jesus and the Kingdom of God), that is great. If you are cold (far from

124

the things of God), at least He can work with you and bring you to salvation, therefore setting you on fire (hot) for His Kingdom. However, when you choose, out of your own volition, to be neither hot or cold, trying to play both sides, He is almost (He is warning you) done with you. But don't push the envelope any further, or you will face your own demise. Listen, my brothers and sisters—and I am speaking to myself, too—you cannot wear the jersey of the Dallas Cowboys but play on the side of the Minnesota Vikings. It wouldn't work. Both teams would drive you away. Today, many reborn Christians are doing this because of pressure from peers, work, and society, not wanting to be ostracized for standing for God and His Kingdom. God understands the enormous pressure you are facing in this age. God empathizes with you. His Son, Jesus, warned us ahead of time in His Word so that we would not falter, because God loves us so dearly. It is written: "'I have told you these things, so that in me you may have peace. In this world you will have trouble. But take heart! I have overcome the world" (Jn 16:33 NIV).

Despite all the entertainment the world today has to offer, it is clear that all is not well. Satan, who is the god of this age, seeks to lure as many people as he can into his camp through deception. This is how he got Eve and eventually Adam, as Eve gave the fruit to Adam, therefore disobeying God. Satan is using the same strategy now. But we have the Bible, the Word of God that warns about Satan's bait and how we should not fall for it. We all sometimes give in to the desires of the flesh and follow its desires and thoughts. But because God is rich in mercy, He made us alive with Christ even when we were dead in our transgressions. So God wants to extend His loving Grace to this generation. The Word says, "... in the coming ages he might show the incomparable riches of his grace, expressed in his kindness to us in Christ Jesus..." (Eph 2:6 NIV).

125

We are His, and He would go to great lengths to protect us without superseding our own will to be away from Him. Today, God is asking you not to abandon Him or what you learned when you were a kid about Him, His Son, and His Kingdom. Return, my dear, back to your first love, and God will embrace you with open arms. We know that because of the great trials and tribulations coming on the earth before Christ returns, it is important to stay anchored to the truth of God's Word. Angels will be sent by the Holy Spirit to shield you from what is to come. We are very close to the end times, and now is not the time to play footsie with the Lord. Choose this day whom you will serve.

I have intentionally included certain topics you might have heard Christians talk about, or maybe you heard about them in a movie, in discussions on social media, or even in the mainstream news. I am referring to the topics of rapture and tribulation. I want to expatiate on these two topics so that you are up to speed on what is unfolding around us. This explanation is primarily for those reading this book who are clueless, for lack of a better word. If you are unfamiliar with them, it might be challenging to understand what is expected to take place before Jesus Christ returns. I want you to know how, by God's grace, you might partake in the rapture or survive the tribulation should you be on the earth when it comes. This brief writing will help you understand the big picture of the end times. It will give you a greater perspective and understanding of the book of Revelation when you read it, and I highly recommend you do read it. Quite frankly, it is not an option considering the recent Coronavirus pandemic. It will also help you enjoy reading the latter part of this book, as many of the things I discuss draw directly from the book of Revelation. Led by the Spirit of God, I am going to define these words in the simplest possible terms rather than giving you some scholarly description.

Rapture: This is when Christians go into the air to heaven after the reborn Christians who have gone before them (already dead and buried) have risen from their graves. How will this happen? It will be possible because God, in His infinite wisdom, will literally transform our bodies into glorified bodies that can move through different mediums at breakneck speed. Just like the movie *Star Trek*, where people move from one medium to another. In the twinkling of an eye, our mortal bodies will be transformed into immortal bodies. The Apostle Paul of Tarsus explains it in first Thessalonians.

It is written: "According to the Lord's word, we tell you that we who are still alive, who are left until the coming of the Lord, will certainly not precede those who have fallen asleep. For the Lord himself will come down from heaven, with a loud command, with the voice of the archangel and with the trumpet call of God, and the dead in Christ will rise first. After that, we who are still alive and are left will be caught up together with them in the clouds to meet the Lord in the air. And so we will be with the Lord forever" (1Thes 4:15-17 NIV).

This isn't science fiction; it is an event that is going to take place whether you choose to believe it or not. This solemn truth should encourage you to be reborn if you are not yet reborn. Jesus gave us an example when He rose from the dead. He had a supernatural body that defied human logic, gravity, and resistance in the atmospheric domain. The Bible tells us He appeared to some 500 people in a span of forty days, and on several occasions He moved through walls to introduce Himself to the disciples after He rose from the dead.

It is written: "Then the same day at evening, being the first day of the week, when the doors were shut where the disciples were assembled for fear of the Jews, came Jesus and stood in the midst, and saith unto them, Peace be unto you. And when he had so said, he shewed unto them his hands and his side. Then were the disciples glad, when they saw the LORD" (Jn 20:19-20 KJV).

Jesus had a powerful glorified body that could never rot or decay, and He will give you that body on the day of rapture. Jesus was promised that kind of body 1,000 years before he came to the earth. David, the giant killer, was not just the king of Israel 1,000 years before Jesus was born in Bethlehem; he was also a poet, a psalmist, and a prophet. He echoed sayings that might have appeared strange then, but it was the spirit of God speaking through David about how Jesus' body had not been allowed to rot or face any form of decay.

It is written: "Therefore my heart is glad, and my glory rejoiceth: my flesh also shall rest in hope. For thou wilt not leave my soul in hell; neither wilt thou suffer thine Holy One to see corruption" (Ps 16:9-10 KJV).

We know King David, who was a prophet, was not speaking of himself because he did die and was buried on Mount Zion, and with time that body decayed. The tomb of David is still in Israel today. So one can confirm what I wrote. He was referring to Jesus, whose body did not see decay or rot, because He rose from the dead. Jesus received an everlasting reward, and that was to sit at the right hand of the Father, far above all principalities, powers, dominions, and names. And God put all things under His feet and made Him the head over all things of the Church, which is Christ's body. So it goes without saying that when you harass or persecute the Church, watch out! You are on dangerous ground, as you are persecuting Jesus Christ.

Tribulation: This will take place during a period that is known as the end times. It is a period in the not too distant future—or maybe even much closer than we are aware—when God, in his anger against the world of unbelievers, will unleash unprecedented hardships on the earth, directed at those who allowed the spirit of the antichrist to convince them not to embrace Jesus Christ and those who rebelled from the Kingdom of God on the earth. Just when the people of the world think everything is fine and dandy, one disaster after another will befall the earth.

There is still a big, healthy debate on whether the reborn will be on Earth when the tribulation takes place. Some believe they will be raptured before it takes place. Others say they will be raptured when the antichrist has been identified (mid-tribulation period), and some say they will go through it—they would be martyrs among the reborn, but none of the reborn would be affected by the punishing plagues, disasters, global hunger, and pandemics so long as they do not have the mark of the beast. This is a chip or tiny device that is placed in the right hand or forehead. Without this chip it would be impossible to trade, buy gas, fly anywhere, board a train, etc. One thing is for sure: It won't be long before we find out how close we are to this period, so there is no time to second-guess this truth. It will not benefit you. Instead, now is the time to deepen your walk with God and draw closer to Him.

Watch out for the number seven, which means completion in the Bible. In the book of Revelation, Jesus appeared in a vision to John on the island of Patmos, where John was incarcerated for sharing the gospel. Jesus held seven stars in his right hand, and He was standing in the middle of seven lampstands. During the period of tribulation, there will be three sets of seven punishing events unleashed on the earth. There will be seven seals, seven trumpet blast by the angels of God, and seven angels who bring seven plagues. The immense suffering during the tribulation will come in the form of plagues, pandemics, wars, and natural disasters. Chapter six of the book of Revelation even talks about the wild beast of the earth. I am wondering whether a new class of animals will suddenly appear on the earth.

Of course, the world, in ignorance, will blame all of these disasters on global warming and aliens. The Christians will be raptured before this horrific experience that the

129

world is unprepared for. In that time many will begin to believe something is not right and will try to give their lives to Jesus Christ, but they will not be able to, as they will have the mark of the beast on their bodies. The Bible says they kept worshiping idols and demons and never repented. The Bible told about these events long before global warming entered the English language. Before the end times kick in, the natural disasters will begin to get intense and more deadly on a global level. The scale and magnitude of these disasters, especially the earthquakes and droughts, will be far greater than people have ever witnessed. In the course of this very terrible nightmare, disasters and cataclysmic weather patterns, as well as war, will cause the world to lose one-third or more of its population. Right now it seems insane almost inconceivable that this will happen. Yet I tell you, my brothers and sisters in Christ, I would rather not enter into a nebulous debate with you over whether this is true. I would prefer for you to enter into a close union with God through His Son, Jesus Christ, so you, too, will escape the mayhem that is to befall the earth.

This is certain to take place because almost everything written in the Bible has come to pass, and this is something that even the most avowed atheist cannot contend with. The predictions in the Bible remain the most powerful difference between it and other religious books. I do not see people verbally attacking or questioning the Koran in the way the media implicitly question the Bible. The Bible is filled with all manner of treasures. It is packed with wisdom, waiting for anyone willing to meditate on the words within it. Unfortunately, many Christians are too busy or disinterested to make time to read the Word of God. They do not realize what a powerful sword they have in their hands. It can protect them; fortify them; wage war, if necessary; and shield them and their loved ones from the activities of the invisible fallen angels who hate us with a passion and know that time is short. These fallen angels are working with their human proxies, who, in most cases, tend to be more disciplined than the regular Christian today. They spend a lot of time questioning the teachings of Jesus on mainstream media. King David, the second ruler of Israel, relied on God's Word to help him achieve his goal of becoming king of Israel. In the book of Psalms, David shared with us how much he relied on God's Word to prevent him from going astray.

It is written: "Your word is a lamp to my feet And a light to my path" (Ps 119:105 AMP).

It is written: "Forever, O LORD, Your word is settled in heaven [standing firm and unchangeable]" (Ps 119:89 AMP).

It is written: "I have better understanding *and* deeper insight than all my teachers [because of Your word]…" (Ps 119:99 AMP).

We are beginning to see some of the things Jesus mentioned in the Bible come to pass. He made mention of what he called "birth pangs." I believe, deep in my heart, that we are beginning to see the birth pangs that a few years away from the actual tribulation period. Take the unexpected Coronavirus pandemic as an example.

It is written: "For nation will rise against nation, and kingdom against kingdom, and there will be famines and earthquakes in various places. But all these things are *merely* the beginning of birth pangs [of the intolerable anguish and the time of unprecedented trouble]" (Mt 24:7-8 AMP).

In the physical, Covid-19 originated from the wet market in Wuhan, China, or in a lab that is underwritten by Canada, the U.S., and the WHO. In the spiritual realm, Satan won permission to bring this disaster on mankind. The devil, with a few exceptions, is the spiritual force behind every major pain and affliction that affects millions of people globally. The real battles are fought in the invisible realm. We affect the outcome by our prayers and our avoidance of the things God hates. The spiritual realm—the invisible realm where all things are formed first— is far more important than what we observe in the physical daily.

It is written, "And they overcome him by the blood of the Lamb, and by the word of their testimony; and they loved not their lives unto the death" (Rv 12:11 KJV). We win our battles in heaven before they arrive on earth, and we do this through intercessory prayers on bended knees. The United States, China, and many nations in Western Europe need to repent. The Church should not assume they will be spared if they keep acting up, for judgment will first begin in the house of God.

Covid-19 was no surprise to God, the twenty-four elders in heaven, or the myriad of angels who worship God in heaven. In fact, it was unfortunately a decision made in heaven to make the pandemic happen. There were no people on Earth with the spirit of Moses who could call off this pandemic before it started in Wuhan, China. If there were, they would have done it. Yes, I understand there was a prophesy years back that said New York's bars and restaurants would shut down for a period, but there was no prophet like Daniel on the ground. Daniel understood the times and seasons he was in; therefore, he often tried to intercede on behalf of the Jewish people who were in exile. God works often with his prophets on ground to ensure His perfect will is established.

It is written: "And we know that in all things God works for the good of those who love him, who have been called according to his purpose" (Romans 8:28 NIV).

Nothing can happen on Earth without the watchful eyes of Jehovah El Roi, the God who sees. It was a warning shot from on high for us to get our acts together. It was a direct message to the world, telling us to seriously consider abandoning the wicked things that are taking place in the open and in the dark in America and the world at large. Both Chinese and Americans have some dark things they are engaging in that have angered the Lord. I would boldly,

132

fearlessly articulate it on the pulpit or during the speaking tour for this book.

One of the clear signs that a country is losing its special relationship with God is when the so-called experts in the country go about tackling a national crisis without applying wisdom. This is especially true when the answer to the problem is right in front of them, and yet they ignore it, to their own peril.

Of course, there are always a few who, through God's grace and the Holy Spirit, will be able to grab hold of the truth and benefit from it. Our socalled experts have denied the tremendous benefit of using hydroxychloroquine to combat Covid-19. They have used the mainstream media to falsely justify their actions. Yet I am here to tell you that nothing has changed in the world since times past. This always happens when people reject God, even when He warns them, they refuse to listen. But God is a merciful God, and He doesn't want anyone die needlessly. He loves you and me, and His desire is for us to discover our purpose and glorify His name while living life abundantly.

When Jesus came on the scene more than 2,000 years ago, the Pharisees and Sadducees, who were supposed to have recognized Jesus, allowed their fear that Jesus would gain more attention than them cloud their judgment. They loathed the fact that He could perform miracles when they couldn't. They saw that He spoke as a brilliant teacher with authority. Demons bowed before Him before He cast them out of people. Amazing grace was displayed. The Pharisees and Sadducees had eyes but could not see, and thus they failed to recognize the Son of man. When the Jewish leaders rejected the Messiah they had been waiting for, He told His disciples that in the not too distant future, they would be invaded by the Romans, and the beautiful temple they had built and were so proud of would be a pile of rubble. Guess what, America. It surely came to pass. Israel suffered immensely from that invasion. The war atrocities the Roman legions carried out on Israel were impossible to describe in words.

Today, they are 195 countries in the world. All of them are giving their patients hydroxychloroquine mixed with some other antiviral cocktails, and the results are encouraging and amazingly positive. Thousands of lives are being saved. In France there is a 91% recovery rate with this drug. Just recently, the government of Great Britain put out a bid to manufacture tons of hydroxychloroquine for its citizens. Yet America has been held hostage by Dr. Fauci, the FDA, and the CDC. While this drug has been available on request thanks to President Trump, there are still thousands of Americans who won't take it and would rather die because they believe the exaggerated lie of the side effects. They are waiting for approval from the FDA before they feel safe to take it. This is because they have been brainwashed by mainstream media, who prefer to talk more about the side effects than the real-life stories of people who have recovered. Yet doctors who have been infected with the virus, along with state representative Karen Whitsett of Michigan, took hydroxychloroquine as a remedy, and their lives were spared. Thank you, God, for providing the wisdom to use hydroxychloroquine and not listen to the naysayers on the news. Because our country is unfortunately divided politically, the mainstream media that support the Democratic party will never show these great testimonies of how hydroxychloroquine has saved lives. No one can point to a patient of Covid-19 who has died of heart problems because they took hydroxychloroquine as a treatment, as it has never happened.

Instead, Dr. Fauci—God bless his heart—is promoting another drug that will cost $700 dollars rather than the twenty dollars you would spend on hydroxychloroquine. The remdesivir drug that Dr. Fauci is promoting has not and will never have the rigorous testing that hydroxychloroquine has had for over fifty years. The president of the United

States has the best healthcare in the world. He has the best doctors tending to his healthcare needs because he is the president of the most powerful country on Earth. In his desperate attempt to educate millions of Americans still wary of taking hydroxychloroquine, he finally told the media he has been taking it at the height of this pandemic. He has been surrounded by staff members who were infected with Covid-19, and he previously did not wear gloves or a mask, except for a few instances, such as when he went to the Ford plant in Michigan. Yet he has tested negative five times. So, what more evidence do you need to figure out who is telling you the truth?

Recently, a well-established pediatrician in Houston, Texas, who also treats Covid-19 patients went public about the 400 patients she had treated with hydroxychloroquine, zinc, and zeta cocktail. She joined several other doctors who have treated Covid-19 patients with hydroxychloroquine and other medicines and have had no deaths recorded among their patients. Other remedies include using an asthma medicine, a nebulizer, and zinc, which was discovered by the doctor in San Antonio. Dr. Stella Immanuel of Houston highlighted the fact that none of her Covid-19 patients had died, and they recovered in a timelier manner than other treatments mandated by the federal government Covid-19 task force. This was an answer to prayers, as more doctors are about to speak out with boldness. Since I was deeply troubled about the rumors regarding the suppression of other remedies for Covid-19, I began to call on the name of the Lord for answers. The Holy Spirit then gave me a very powerful Scripture found in the Bible, which allowed me to petition God to reveal the truth pertaining to hydroxychloroquine and the opposition by Dr. Fauci, CNN, Facebook's Mark Zuckerberg, and the mainstream media. God assured me through His Spirit that He would give this issue no rest until the truth comes out.

135

This is what the word of God says: "There is nothing concealed that will not be disclosed, or hidden that will not be made known. What you have said in the dark will be heard in the daylight, and what you have whispered in the ear in the inner rooms will be proclaimed from the roofs" (Lk 12:2-3 NIV). The spiritual power behind this Scripture has begun to yield great dividends physically in terms of exposing hidden secrets pertaining to Covid-19.

Dr. Immanuel went so far as to call the combined medicine a prevention of Covid-19. No one dared to question her stunning results and breakthroughs. All they did was criticize her deliverance ministry in regard to casting out unclean spirits from people, as she was also a pastor of a church. I asked God why there was suppression of the truth of hydroxychloroquine being another form of treatment for Covid. He said powerful people in both the government and the private sector in the country would rather allow people to die for political, financial, and economic reasons than give them the medicine, unlike other countries, which have given their people the medicine to overcome this pandemic. This will lead to an uproar in America, especially among African Americans, many of whom have fallen sick and died from this pandemic.

It is written: "My people are destroyed for lack of knowledge..." (Hos 4:6 KJV).

God is telling you through His Word that people die needlessly because they don't have the right information. The key word is "right." The mainstream media, unfortunately, have become the main supporter of one of the two political parties, and the news outlets have backed Dr. Fauci rather than vigorously question him. Meanwhile, Americans have died from the Coronavirus even though they could have been saved from it. They also want to promote a vaccine, which will be a big moneymaking machine for whoever develops one. Some Americans have forgotten we have had flu vaccines available every year for several decades. Yet

136

each year over one hundred thousand Americans, including both children and adults, die from the flu. Millions, by the Grace of God, recover from it. So, it goes without saying that having a vaccine to mitigate the spread of Covid-19 would not be a silver bullet, as people today are still dying from the flu even though there is a vaccine. My faith is in God's divine protection because I know Him, not a vaccine, although it would be a welcome development and a breakthrough to have a vaccine for Covid-19 ready by the fall. At least it would begin to stop the fear millions of Americans have of Covid-19, which has swallowed their joy and paralyzed their ability to enjoy their lives abundantly, as Jesus would want them to do despite Covid-19. Don't fear Covid-19; fear God. The Bible tells us, "The angel of the LORD encamps around those who fear him, and he delivers them" (Ps 34:7 NIV). In a nutshell, God will protect us and have His angels shield those who show their reverential respect for Him by their obedience to His Word and their uncompromising fidelity to the things of God.

The stock market went up today because a company announced some clinical trial success. The FDA-approved remdesivir drug success ratio is very small. It would reduce recovery from Covid-19 from fifteen days to eleven days. Hydroxychloroquine just got axed again by the FDA because they said the risk outweighed the benefits. This was a shock to me because I took this drug as a kid many times to ensure I did not catch malaria. To this day, no American has died from complications relating to hydroxychloroquine while being treated for Covid-19, and Dr. Fauci knowns this.

The mainstream news has outright refused to show the testimonies of those who have taken this drug and recovered faster. I believe the best way to solve the question about this drug is to do a test case. Take ten people, or even 100, who have Covid-19. Give one group the treatment recommended by the FDA, and give the other group hydroxychloroquine. Then we can look at the results. I bet the FDA would say no to this test. Yet this is how people from the Bible solved problems when it came to deciding whose god was greater—the God of Elijah or the god of Baal. We know the end of that story.

If what they say is true about its danger to the human heart, why are kids in Africa who take this medicine still alive today? I believe that, more than any other available drug today, it will do a better job at helping a patient with Covid-19 than any other drug. God sees all of this, and it grieves Him to see what is going on. He will not sit idle for long. His hand is being restrained by the righteous who continue to lift America in prayer. God is a faithful, covenant-keeping God. When a life is lost that could have been saved, it hurts the family that lost the loved one, but it also hurts God. The Bible tells us that it isn't the desire of the Father in heaven for even a wicked person to perish.

It is written: "Again and Again they put God to test; they vexed the Holy One of Israel. They did not remember his power..." (Ps 78:41-42 NIV).

God is demonstrating His great love for America and the world at large. He is saving millions of lives worldwide out of His abundant mercy. The mainstream news did a good job warning us about Covid-19, but they may have unintentionally spread the spirit of fear that killed more people than the virus itself. When a person's spirit is weak and dead, nothing else can sustain the flesh. This is why the Bible tells us, "...guard your heart, for everything you do flows from it" (Prv 4:23 NIV). Fear is a powerful spirit, and the Bible speaks about it. Once fear takes deep root in your heart, you become vulnerable to all kinds of diseases. You experience a nervous breakdown. You have anxiety attacks. Your immune system goes into disarray rather than focusing on fighting the virus. Your white and red blood cells are weakened by fear and thus do not put up much of a resistance to this virus. Unknown to most people who are not Christians, fear is a spirit, and it is from Satan.

It is the opposite of bold faith, which is from God. God protected millions of Americans from catching this virus. When all is said and done and this virus has been subdued, there will be a spike because more people will be exposed and will then test positive. What we are now all realizing is that being outside actually builds your immune system to the virus. This is why, when people who have hardly left the house start going out, their immune systems won't be as strong the immune systems of the people who have been outside.

You may ask me how I know for sure that God limited the spread of the virus in the world and put His protection around His chosen few. It is not rocket science. The news is finally reporting that there were far more Americans and who didn't get the virus citizens of the world who were exposed and didn't get the virus than there were of those who did. A lot of people had antibodies to this virus. Our immune systems, which were provided by God Himself, kicked in and kicked Covid-19 out. Hallelujah! Give God great praise. He also largely kept this virus from affecting many children and young adults. Yes, some children got Covid-19, but that number was very small.

The flu has, in the past, been devasting for kids as well as adults. But this was not the case with the Coronavirus. There is a great mystery in this. Children, to a large extent, are innocent in the eyes of God until they get to an age of understanding right and wrong. Also, the young adults who were partying at various beaches in America were protected, with the exception of a few, because the knowledge of the things of God has not been handed over to them like it has been in the past. God's mercy has again been extended. This mercy of God was provided even though their parents did not spend time instructing them on the Word of God and the things that pertain to godliness and good living. Amazingly, the Father of amazing grace plans to use these same people He spared to glorify His name. What a mighty

God we serve. You are about to witness a mighty move of His spirit flow through His people. It is out of these people that a great revival will arise in America. God is going to use our youth, who are currently tied to the things of the world, to glorify His name in a big way in America, and it will spread like wildfire all over the world. It is called the Great Awakening.

It is written: "It shall come about after this That I shall pour out My Spirit on all mankind; And your sons and your daughters will prophesy, Your old men will dream dreams, Your young men will see visions" (Jl 2:28 AMP).

Many have said this prophesy was fulfilled when Peter spoke after the day of Pentecost. But the Scriptures refer to young men seeing visions, not just older men like Peter. This has already begun and will reach an accelerated pace before the end of this year. Secondly, the prophesy says God will pour out His spirit on all mankind, not just the 120 at Pentecost, many of whom were Israelites.

Do not ever forget that God loves America and that the Great Awakening, which will sweep through the whole world, is coming. Meanwhile, God has provided a Bible for us so we can learn from the consequences Israelites face any time they strayed from God's path. No amount of grace can erase the truth that God disciplines those whom He loves. There were no ten commandments when He sent burning Sulphur against Sodom and Gomorrah. In fact, it was during the time when grace was in full force— evidenced by the fact that He took an unbeliever, a Chaldean, where there were idol worshipers, and He brought Abraham out of that land and turned his heart toward God, then poured a generational blessing on him—when He called Abraham His friend and, above all, consulted with Abraham and allowed him to enter negotiations with Him before destroying Sodom and Gomorrah, completely wiping out the city.

On the other hand, many pastors preach on the pulpit that God is not angry with America. With all due respect,

140

I honestly do not know where they get their information from, and quite frankly, it isn't my position to judge. I can only say that I pray they are right. They are far more optimistic than I am. Besides, who am I but a preacher of the gospel? Nevertheless, I do know one thing: Those of you who are parents can be angry with your children when they misbehave, and even though you love them dearly and would lay down your life for them—as Jesus of Nazareth did for all of us—you still discipline them when they misbehave or get out of line. You must, or they would grow to disrespect and even hate you. It is written: "…and you have forgotten the divine word of encouragement which is addressed to you as sons, 'MY SON, DO NOT MAKE LIGHT OF THE DISCIPLINE OF THE LORD, AND DO NOT LOSE HEART *and* GIVE UP WHEN YOU ARE CORRECTED BY HIM; FOR THE LORD DISCIPLINES *and* CORRECTS THOSE WHOM HE LOVES, AND HE PUNISHES EVERY SON WHOM HE RECEIVES *and* WELCOMES [TO HIS HEART]'" (Heb 12:5-6 AMP).

If our earthly parents can scold us when we are out of order, how can we expect our Heavenly Father to do any less? If our earthly parents can get angry with us when we do something egregiously wrong, why is it that God can't get upset? Although my father spanked me when I misbehaved, it does not mean he never loved me. Was Jesus not upset when He drove the money changers and people selling pigeons out of the temple in Jerusalem? In the book of Acts, Ananias and Sapphira, his wife, literally dropped dead for lying to Peter about putting the wrong amount of money in the offering. Saints, this was the New Testament, and Jesus had risen from the dead. If the Ruach HaKodesh, the Holy Spirit, did not want them dead, they wouldn't have died that way.

It is written: "What made you think of doing such a thing? You have not lied just to human beings but to God.' When Ananias heard this, he fell down and died. And great fear seized all who heard what had happened... About three hours later his wife came in, not knowing what had happened. Peter asked her, 'Tell me, is this the price you and Ananias got for the land?' 'Yes,' she said, 'that is the price.' Peter said to her, 'How could you conspire to test the Spirit of the Lord? Listen! The feet of the men who buried your husband are at the door, and they will carry you out also.' At that moment she fell down at his feet and died" (Acts 5:4-10 NIV).

Paul of Tarsus, the writer of the grace message in the Bible, was upset when he said, "You foolish Galatians! Who has bewitched you?" (Gal 3:1 NIV). He said this when they tried to mix the law with grace. Jesus is the lamp of God, and He takes the away the sins of the world, but on another hand, He is judge of all and the lion of the tribe of Judah. God has wrath, but His grace keeps it from being aimed at mankind. However, there is an appointed time for Him to act if His warnings have not caused us to turn from our wicked ways. Pastors do not preach this kind of message in churches these days because they are not hearing from God. There is an even more painful virus that is coming, and doctors and scientists will be clueless on how to deal with it. A lockdown will not help at all. Let us all go on bended knees now and worship the God of our founding fathers.

It is written: "It is you alone who are to be feared. Who can stand before you when you are angry? From heaven you pronounced judgment, and the land feared and was quiet — when you, God, rose up to judge, to save all the afflicted of the land. Surely your wrath against mankind brings you praise, and the survivors of your wrath are restrained" (Ps 76:7-10 NIV).

Yes, God gives all of us a long rope and is most reluctant to punish us. Even in the Tanakh, God was reluctant to punish Kind David when he sinned, but when He did, He did with mercy. So please, please search the Scriptures before saying God doesn't get angry when we deliberately and consciously disobey him and engage in things He hates. God is sending a very powerful message for all of us to enter into repentance while we still have time. He expects us, the reborn, to lead by example by doing away with the sins of the heart that most easily entangle us. You know why? Because judgment will first begin in the house of God. Isn't this true? God tells us this in the Bible, so let's stop pretending. Remember that Jesus Christ is the same yesterday, today, and forever (Heb 13:8).

If you are a Christian, do you remember the Lord's prayer? "…Thy will be done in earth, as it is in heaven" (Mt 6:10 KJV). This means you must be victorious in heaven before you can see the victory on Earth, and prayer is your weapon. Remember the story of Daniel in the lion's den. This has been documented historically, not just biblically. Before ISIS, the terrorist group, destroyed the artifacts, rich history, and culture of Iraq, all the historical truth of Daniel was there, even under the late dictator Saddam Hussein. He was of the Muslim faith, but he saw that it was important to preserve that cultural history. When he was overthrown, all of that was lost, and what was not destroyed was illegally auctioned off to the highest bidder. ISIS had the spirit of the antichrist, because they destroyed the very things that could prove to the Iraqi Muslims, and the entire Arab population, that the God of Daniel is the one true God and that every other god on Earth is an idol.

It is written: "Sing to the LORD, all the earth; proclaim his salvation day after day. Declare his glory among the nations, his marvelous deeds among all peoples. For great is the LORD and most worthy of praise; he is to be feared above all gods. For all the gods of the nations are idols…" (1 Chr 16:23-26 NIV). How things unfold on Earth in the physical isn't as important than the fact it was decided in the third heavens and even worse allowed to occur when it is detrimental to our interest. This is a powerful sign of the weakness of the Church globally. Churches are getting bigger and bigger state-of-the-art buildings, but there is a deflated spiritual power. It is our actions on Earth that strengthen the hand of our number one adversary, the devil. God did not necessarily do this. After all, Satan is the god of this age. Instead, God is the ultimate healer, and He restores health and has been hearing the prayers of the righteous to end the Coronavirus. The fact that it occurred isn't as damning as the disruption it has caused in our economy and way of life. This Coronavirus dealt a temporary blow to all the idols the American people have had as a result of a booming economy. Our fellow Americans who have these idols may not even be aware that they have them. It is fair to say that most of us, especially those who are not reborn, would rather gamble and lose money in the casinos of the world than put money in the Church or toward a good cause, such as the fight to end child sexual molestation. Child prostitution is now a global pandemic worse than the Coronavirus. The idols of today are different from the voodoo dolls and the other gods the Israelites had. (Joshua was the war general of Israel and was used by God to bring down the wall Jericho spoke to the Israelites about before he passed away.)

It is written: "Now therefore fear the LORD, and serve him in sincerity and in truth: and put away the gods which your fathers served on the other side of the flood, and in Egypt; and serve ye the LORD. And if it seem evil unto you to serve the LORD, choose you this day whom ye will serve; whether the gods which your fathers served that were on the other side of the flood, or the gods of the Amorites, in whose land ye dwell: but as for me and my house, we will serve the LORD" (Jo 24:14-15 KJV).

Modern day idols have indeed taken a different form. It is no secret that other nations of the earth choose to worship other, lifeless gods. I understand that they are working with artificial intelligence to rectify that problem. Some of these are the large statues you see in foreign nations that they

144

call gods that according to Psalm 115 in the bible, not me but what the Jews that wrote the bible say and I agree with them.

It is written: "They have mouths, but they speak not: eyes have they, but they see not: They have ears, but they hear not: noses have they, but they smell not: They have hands, but they handle not: feet have they, but they walk not: neither speak they through their throat" (Ps 115:5-7 KJV).

The idols in America, Western Europe, and the emerging economies of the world are more sophisticated, and they're rampant, even among reborn Christians. An idol is anything you are obsessed with or engage with often. This can be many things, including sports, gambling, partying, news, and social media. Some of us are addicted to watching sports on our smartphones, televisions, and laptops. I understand that we sometimes all need to rest and do something relaxing or entertaining. Nevertheless, it should not be done at the expense of the quality time God wants to have with you. God could need to warn you of an impending danger that is headed your way, but you are too busy to get the message before something unfortunate happens.

God wants to talk to you and me more than we care to know. He does this often through the Holy Spirit, who speaks directly to your heart but is not in any way limited to this method of communication. When you are not listening, it can shortchange your life on Earth. This nearly happened to me because I was married to my job. Yes, it was an idol in my life. I was involved in an accident that nearly cost me my life, and it took two years for me to fully recover. Two weeks before the accident, a devout man of God visited my workplace and warned me that I needed to start working on the things God had called me to do and that perilous times were ahead for me. He said he had been praying for me and he felt sure that I needed to enter a special time of prayer and consecration with God. I took him at his word, but I cannot recall praying about it. This was a hard lesson I had to learn.

Other times God wants to talk to you because there is an opportunity coming your way that God, who loves you, does not want you to miss it. This could be an opportunity for God to impart wisdom and direction to you in order to make you a successful entrepreneur for the Kingdom of God, but you are too occupied with other things to tune into the frequency of heaven and hear what He has to say. The idols of the heart block our ability to hear what the spirit of the Lord is saying to us.

We are a blessed nation, and God has been very good to America for over two centuries. Yet none of these things should have usurped our relationship with God. We should know the truth by now: God is not against having fun, shopping, going to movies, texting, social media, or anything that brings temporary happiness to our hearts. It was Jesus who said, "...I am come that they may have life, and that they may have it more abundantly" (Jn 10:10 KJV). Jesus was the embodiment of having a good time and having fun. In fact, He turned everything into a wonderful experience. Even when death was in the homes of certain individuals, He rose them from the dead, and rejoicing swept the entire community. He laid hands on the sick, and they recovered. He commanded demons out of people, and the families rejoiced and worshiped Him.

When they ran out of wine at a wedding party at Cana in Galilee, it was Jesus who stepped in to ameliorate the situation by literally changing water into wine. And yes, if you search the Scriptures, there is a hint that the wine had some alcohol. The Bible says that when they ran out of the good wine and the people had had quite a bit, they served the cheap wine. Why is that? Common sense would tell any reader it was because the drunks usually wouldn't be able to differentiate between the good wine and the cheap wine, nor

146

would they care. But in reality, the problem they had at this wedding was that they had they ran out of wine completely. Not even cheap wine was available until the Son of God— the Savior, the Messiah, the Son of righteousness, the Son of the Highest, Yeshua—stepped in and intervened. This act done by Jesus has never been replicated by anyone on Earth that I know of. Jesus knew that if they were not able to come up with more wine, it would have been an embarrassment that would've lasted a long time. The family of the couple would've been gossiped about and ridiculed in Galilee. Jesus attended another major celebration with His disciples when Levi, a customs official and tax collector, invited Jesus to his mansion. The Bible says Levi threw a great feast for Jesus and His disciples.

It is written: "And the Pharisees and their scribes grumbled at his disciples, saying, 'Why do you eat and drink with tax collectors and sinners?' And Jesus answered them, 'Those who are well have no need of a physician, but those who are sick. I have not come to call the righteous but sinners to repentance'" (Lk 5:30-32 ESV).

Jesus turned everything into a celebration, and the Bible notes several great feasts that Jesus was part of. At Zacchaeus's house the party was even bigger. He often stayed at Martha and Mary's vineyard, a large mansion and compound. In fact, it was Lazarus, Martha, and Mary's brother, whom Jesus rose from the dead after a brief illness, that triggered the high priest's plan to kill Jesus. When He met Mary Magdalene, the woman Jesus cast seven demons out of, it was at a high priest's house, where He was having lunch. Jesus had compassion on the poor, the sick, the destitute, and the little fellows of society, but He also ministered to the Rockefellers in His time, as they, too, were in need of salvation and more than likely had the money to fund His ministry. When Jesus died, the spices they used on His body and the clothing for His burial were funded and provided by two multi-millionaires: Joseph of Arimathea, secret disciple of Jesus, and Nicodemus, a high priest who was believed to be the third richest man in Israel at that time.

Let Us Pray

Righteous and holy God, hallow by thy name. Be thou exalted, O God, above the heavens, and let thy glory be above all the earth. We thank You for being a good, good Father. Do not rebuke us in Your anger or chasten us in Your hot displeasure; have mercy on us. Strengthen us on the inside so that we may have the fortitude and mindset to do away with the idols of this world, which lead us away from the things of God. We make a heartfelt decision today, this very moment, to draw closer to You in Jesus' name. Enable us through Your Holy Spirit to be Kingdomminded, abandoning the world of pride, the lust of the flesh, and vain gloriousness. As we draw closer to You, You will draw closer to us so that we may resist the devil and force him to flee from us. Finally, empower us to prioritize fellowship with You and to worship You daily in spirt and in truth. In Jesus' name I pray. Amen.

Chapter 7

AS THE NATIONS OF THE WORLD TURN

As I was writing this book, I looked at my smartphone, and YouTube had recommended a video of a sermon given by a preacher in Texas. With no disrespect to this erudite pastor, I had never really heard of him. The sermon had been given several years ago. Within a few minutes of listening to this message on YouTube, I realized this Baptist minister was one of the rare ministers of the gospel who did not sugarcoat his message to soothe the itchy ears of audiences in America and throughout the world, who want to hear anything but the truth these days. He brilliantly articulated a message that was reminiscent of the late Dr. Martin Luther King in style, skill, and delivery. He made a favorable impression on me, and it got me stirred up because this man of God was echoing a message that had been on my heart for a very long time.

In summary, the preacher echoed the truth that it takes only a quarter of a century for this generation to forget where we came from and what God has done for us as a country. We all know that this is possible if we do not instruct our kids on how God has been merciful to us. The incoming generation will be clueless and will not know why it is important to adhere to the teachings of the gospel. They will not know about the wisdom it provides on how to live a godly, quiet life of peace and prosperity. You may say, "Wait a second, Peter. This is impossible. After all, we are in the information age, and any information we desire is literally at our fingertips." This is true, but we all forget one thing: The ability to receive information readily was predicted in the Bible by Daniel, the prophet. But the reverse is also very true and disturbing. The same technology can be turned against us and used to monitor everything we do for marketing purposes, and when the time comes, they can be used for persecutorial purposes by dictatorial governments.

Our smartphones have become the greatest legal listening devices in the world. Unless you cut off your communications, you are being listened to not only by "Big Brother," but also by big business that try to hear what you want so they can market to you. When my wife and I want to travel somewhere, we discuss where we want to go, and within an hour we will be getting advertisements for flights, hotels, and vacation packages to the very places we mentioned.

We usually laugh about this, but it's scary that we are so monitored, and this is dangerous for our longterm freedom.

I do not watch that much television or that many movies, but I do like spy movies and intriguing movies involving commandos or special forces. So yes, it is true that I like shows like *Homeland* on *Seal Team*. These two shows will give you a glimpse of what we have gotten ourselves into with technology. At the age of twelve, I was intrigued about foreign policy, so I listened to a lot BBC Radio and Voice of America. I learned about coup d'etat, the CIA, the KGB, MI5, MI6, the Cold War, the Angola Civil War, the difference between Iran and Iraq, and how the Shan of Iran was restored to power in 1958 by the CIA. I knew the difference between the M60 battle tank and the T72 tank of Russia. I knew the benefits of the F-4 Phantom jet verses the MiG 21, 23, and 25, along with the later version of the MIG 29. I knew by the age of fourteen that every embassy had a CIA station chief. I did not need wiki leak to know what was

150

later revealed to the whole world. I could browse through *Time* and *Newsweek* and literally remember everything written in them. Apart from history and foreign policy, I was pretty much an average student in school. Twenty-five years after I was reborn, I became "dangerous" because of the prophetic dreams the Spirit of God imparted into me.

In a nutshell, the same tech giants who gave us our smartphones also have the ability to track what we download, watch, and send to friends on social media. Recently, the president of Ghana—a dignified man of timbre and caliber, a man not given into conspiracy theories but steeped in wisdom and knowledge—allegedly said some pretty interesting and intriguing things about the origins of Covid-19. Later investigation revealed it could be fake news. Keep in mind that he is a president of a country that has friendly relations with the United States. Both former President Obama and President Clinton visited this nation when they were in office. Ghana is relatively prosperous when compared to its other African neighbors. She has a thriving democracy and is rich in oil, gold, cocoa, timber, bauxite, and tourism. Yet because what the moderate president of Ghana said was worrisome to certain powerful people in the world, his broadcast was, within hours, taken off YouTube, Facebook, and other social media outlets. Even the people I sent it to could not send it to other people because the ability to send the link was disabled. How were they able to do this? Regardless of whether the information was authentic or fake, it was scary because they had to have tracked everyone I sent it to. So how is it that social media companies get to now sanction what they deem to be false or truthful, without any oversight to see whether they are engaging in press censorship based on their political party's philosophy or doctrine? About a month ago, my wife, Juanita, wrote this on Facebook: "Melania Trump is one of the most beautiful first ladies we have had in America." Obviously, this was just her opinion and was no big deal. However, I do not necessarily disagree with her. Melania was formerly a model. To our unpleasant surprise, Facebook sent her a note that said this information was not factual and so they were removing it from their platform. We were stunned about this censorship. We could not believe that Facebook would respond to such trivial information. What are they afraid of? This is not hate speech or divisive. It is scary that this is taking place in America. We are slowly becoming like China, and our tech giants are bringing this wicked form of control and manipulation into our country. We all are living in an increasingly falling world, filled with all manner of distractions.

There are many citizens in this country who subscribe to different faiths, and the freedom of religion in this country allows people to practice their faith without fear of persecution by either angry mobs or the government. The early founders of our nation were no doubt inspired by many of the writings in the Holy Scripture. To erase the influence of Christian values in our lives is to erase much of what was written in the Constitution that has governed our nation successfully for many years. The increasingly secularist agenda in our schools has left our kids—and soon it will be our grandkids—with no knowledge whatsoever on how the writers of our cherished Constitution were inspired by the JudeoChristian values they grew up with, nor will they know how good God has been to America despite her shortcomings. We know that there are plans afoot to make a global central government more powerful than ones with faith in God. This will not happen until the antichrist has come onto the world stage.

It is written: "My people, hear my teaching; listen to the words of my mouth. I will open my mouth with a parable; I will utter hidden things, things from of old—things we have heard and known, things our ancestors have told us. We will not hide them from their descendants; we will tell the next generation the praiseworthy deeds of the LORD, his power,

152

and the wonders he has done. He decreed statutes for Jacob and established the law in Israel, which he commanded our ancestors to teach their children, so the next generation would know them, even the children yet to be born, and they in turn would tell their children. Then they would put their trust in God and would not forget his deeds but would keep his commands" (Ps 78:1-7 NIV).

It is no secret that many young adults, including college students whose parents grew up going to church, have just about abandoned the things that pertain to God. The only exceptions are parents who insist their children join them in church on Sundays or at the synagogues on the Sabbath.

Even more worrisome, many of the young adults in America are unaware of the deliberate decision by the founding fathers to use the Bible as a source of inspiration when crafting our cherished Constitution. Today, there is a Bible museum in Washington D.C. that was built at the cost of almost a billion dollars. I haven't yet had the opportunity to visit this supposedly imposing structure. Yet those who have visited this epic building describe it in terms that show that their lives will never be the same after visiting that facility. It validates their belief in the Word of God being a written document from the most high God.

James Madison's quote: "We have staked the whole future of American civilization, not upon power of government, far from it. We gave staked the future of all of our political institutions upon the capacity of mankind for self-government; upon the capacity of each and all of us to govern ourselves, to control ourselves, to sustain ourselves according to the Ten Commandments of God."

While it is true that Jesus Christ fulfilled the law for us and we are now under the grace dispensation, the above-mentioned statement by Madison underscores the desire of our founding fathers to establish a morally righteous government that is answerable to the people.

To the rest of the world, can't you see that even the medical insignia in our hospitals all over America, and even on the insignia and flag of the WHO of the United Nations, comes from the Bible? This symbol is one of a snake around a pole and the map of the world behind it (Nm 21:6-9). It is, after all, the most recognized symbol of healthcare in the world. It was a reminder of the bronze snake Moses, the great Jewish prophet who led the Jews out of the wilderness, placed on the pole so that any Israelite who was bitten by a fiery snakes in the wilderness was spared from death by just looking up at the pole. Just to let you know, they were bitten by snakes because they were complaining and whining about God Almighty, the Hashem. Jesus Christ had not yet come to the world, so they were under the old covenant, and any time they misbehaved, they got spanked by God. When Jesus came, the grace of God allowed Him to overlook the offenses and sins of those who believe Jesus died for our sins more than 2,000 years ago. And to those who are not reborn, God's mercy is still extended until their cup of iniquity, or the nation's cup, is full. Yet let me be clear: God is known for punishing those He loves in order to bring them to order. He does it because He loves you. After all, parents who love their kids still discipline them when it is necessary, appropriate, and imperative.

Nations all over the world—particularly the U.S. and nations in Western Europe that have democracies, freedom of speech, and freedom of religion—will eventually, as foretold in the Bible, begin to persecute the Church. They will use the laws in their land to muzzle the ones who hold on to the Word of God. We live in a world today where the love of self and pleasure is considered more important than the things of God. Thus, it was a breath of fresh air when the Supreme Court, in July of 2020, ruled in favor of religious schools having access to scholarships, just like other private academic institutions. This helps parents fund the education of their kids even if they want to send them to faith-based schools. Just as you see the tearing down of statues all over America to appease a section of our population, so shall Christians find themselves hated by every nation in the world within a few short years. It is coming.

How is this supposed persecution of the Christians going to happen? Well, something is coming that the world will find imperative, but Christians will want nothing to do with it. I am not talking about those who go to church for religious purposes, as there are so many churches in which the Spirit of God is no longer there. I am making reference to those of us who would not allow the laws of the land cause us to disobey God on the things He has discussed in His written Word. The thing that the world will want is going to deceive them, convince them that their very lives depend on it, and make them think that their survival will only be guaranteed if the whole world participates in it. It will be easy to convince the world otherwise because this deception will be orchestrated by the antichrist himself. According to the Word of God, he will be given power to prevail even against the Christians. Family members will become enemies of each other. Nations, in their error and pride, will begin to question what they once believed. They will make a mockery of the same Scriptures their citizens previously evangelized to other nations. They will consciously forget what their founding fathers stood for. They will abrogate the strong traditions and cherished laws that had preserved their democracies and made them prosperous. They will do this by enacting laws that are contrary to what is acceptable to God. Anyone who challenges what they want will be persecuted, severely fined, or incarcerated. Jesus warned us about this long ago, so we shouldn't be unpleasantly surprised. Instead, we need to continue to keep our eyes on Jesus, the author and finisher of our faith.

It is written: "On my account you will be brought before governors and kings as witnesses to them and to the gentiles. But when they arrest you, do not worry about what to say or how to say it. At that time you will be given what to say... You will be hated by everyone because of me, but the one who stands firm to the end will be saved" (Mt 10:18-22 NIV).

In fact, family members will be divided, and many will betray one another just to save their own skin. God is not going to just sit and watch it unfold. He will strike those who carry the mark of the beast with great torment and suffering. For example, there are people within family units today who believe in "marriage equality," that basically says the expansion of marriage laws by the Supreme Court of America is a good thing. There are others in those same family units who believe anything that contradicts and opposes what God declared in His Word. This is flat-out wrong and immoral, and America will face dire consequences spiritually in the near and foreseeable future. These discussions can arouse passion disagreement among brothers and sisters. Jesus, who knew no sin but for our sake became a sin offering, predicted what we are witnessing unfold in some nations of the world today. Keep in mind that there will also be political division, although not mentioned in the Bible, especially if a particular political candidate stands for moral absolutes and biblical principles and another stands for the exact opposite. You will find members of the same family supporting opposing candidates not just because of their political parties but also based on whether they put the Word of God above the law of the land when it comes to moral rectitude. These divisions have already begun, and this is what Jesus has always known. A time is unfortunately coming where it will be increasingly difficult to publicly identify with Christ Jesus and the things of God without facing persecution and intimidation from friends, family, associates, relatives, colleagues, classmates, different organizations, and even the government.

It is written: "'Do not think that I have come to bring peace on the earth; I have not come to bring peace, but

156

a sword [of division between belief and unbelief]. For I have come to SET A MAN AGAINST HIS FATHER, AND A DUGHTER AGAINST HER MOTHER, AND A DAUGHTER-IN-LAW AGAINST HER MOTHER-IN-LAW; and A MAN'S ENEMIES WILL BE THE MEMBERS OF HIS [own] HOUSEHOLD [when one believes and another does not]" (Mt 10:34-36 AMP). Just before Republicans were about to begin their 2020 convention, news came out about President Trump's sister, who was saying some unpleasant things about her brother. This was exactly what Jesus was talking about when He said a man's enemies would be from his own household. Those who oppose the things of God will use the courts in their countries to rule in favor of their agendas, unless the courts are full of judges who rightly believe in the strict interpretation and application of the Constitution. I am sorry to say: This intimidation of the body of Christ has already begun. From Canada to Great Britain to Sweden, the churches and houses of worship are being muzzled. They're being told to comply with laws that have been enacted to limit what the pastor or minister can say while preaching on the pulpit. This is why, in America, there is a great fight about who ascends to the bench of the Supreme Court. In the height of the pandemic, certain states allowed for peaceful and violent demonstrations. Some wore masks, while others did not wear them at all. Yet they say you can't go to church to pray and give thanks to God, even when the churches comply with social distancing and the wearing of masks. Who are they fooling? Certainly not you and me, and certainly not God.

Meanwhile, the emerging democracies in the developing world are moving in the opposite direction. For example, the developing nations in Africa and throughout the world are given freedom of religion. Some of these developing nations are providing greater freedoms to the houses of worship, allowing them to say what they want to say. This is true even when what they say is unpopular and contradictory of government policy. Why the change of heart in the leaders of these developing nations, especially if they are mild dictators and have been put in power without free and fair elections?

It's because the evangelists from the United States, Europe, and the soils of Africa have actively been spreading the gospel there in the last 100 years. The African nations have been hungry for the Word of God. I remember watching Oral Roberts on TV while I was in Africa in the 70s. Then, the main churches were Anglican and Catholic. I loved to see the Spirit of God move in the ministries of Oral Roberts. Trinity Broadcasting Network came along around 1984 and opened up in South Africa. Today, TBN has spread the gospel all over the world. Many emerging nations, from Sri Lanka to Brazil, now have 24/7 access to messages from the Bible. These nations have found the gospel liberating and uplifting. As they have tuned into the gospel, their mindsets have changed about themselves and their lives. From Australia to Africa to South America to Central America, the gospel has been preached through TBN and other Christian TV networks like Daystar.

The non-denomination church, or the reborn church, is now the biggest Christian ministry in Nigeria, Brazil, Indonesia, and even China. There are about a hundred million Christians in China, even with the suppression of religion there. They often meet underground because of Chinese authorities. Before Covid-19, crusades involving the preaching of the gospel can sometimes have an attendance of more than a million in certain parts of Africa. In addition, people who cannot make it to the crusades are able to watch it on television or on their smartphones. Technology has no doubt played a significant role in spreading the gospel to the developing world.

John the Baptist came to fulfill his mission on Earth in the spirit of Elijah, as written in the Bible. Around 800 years before John the Baptist was born to Zacharia and Elizabeth,

158

Isaiah spoke about John, who he was going to be, and how he would come to prepare the way for the coming of the Messiah. It is amazing that the Bible is the only book that mentions people before they are born into this world. This makes the Bible the greatest predictor of events. The CIA, MI5, Russia's SVR and GRU, and the German Federal Intelligence Service cannot match the Bible in its predictive analysis of events before they happen.

The Lord revealed to me that the Spirit of God that was in Paul of Tarsus was placed in Paul Crouch of TBN. Just like Paul of Tarsus, who wrote two-thirds of the New Testament and helped reach the gentiles more than any of the original eleven disciples of Christ, Paul Crouch and his wife, Jan Crouch, went through immense suffering when TBN began in 1973. Yet they remained committed to the divine assignment and the race that was set before them. So, with the exact same Spirit of God that was in Paul of Tarsus in the Bible, Paul Crouch literally fulfilled the spreading of the gospel throughout the world through the television station TBN. Through TBN, the gospel was preached in Farsi to the Iranians and in Arabic to the Middle Eastern nations. With the satellite stations they have acquired all over the earth, TBN and Daystar have their network blanketing literally every nation on Earth. The work done by TBN and other Christian television would have been unimaginable sixty years ago. These networks are unknowingly hastening the return of the Messiah, as He will return when the gospel has been heard all around the world.

It is written: "And this gospel of the kingdom shall be preached in the all the world for a witness unto all nations; and then shall the end come" (Mt 24:14 KJV). These were the exact words of Jesus. Continents like Africa have benefited from devote ministers of the gospel who understood their calling and focused like a laser beam on the assignment God gave them, without deviating to other worldly agendas. So they bore great fruit. One of those ministers was Pastor

159

Enoch Adeboye of the Redeemed Christian Church of God, who went from being a college professor rose to being one of the top 100 most important people in the world, and this was all because of God's grace on his life and over the ministry he was in charge off. Reinhard Bonnke, a late German-born evangelist, was able to go to the predominately Muslim northern part of Nigeria and pull a crowd of a million people to the preaching of the gospel.

Then there is Bishop Oyedepo, a mighty man of valor and wealth, who carries a Davidic, Solomonic, Elijah, and Joshua anointing. He doesn't fear anyone, not even the president in Nigeria, and he calls it like he sees it. As a result, Africa and South America have become the continents that most revere and fear the things of God. The economic growth of these nations has also yielded one of the fastest growth rates among the nations on the earth. Unfortunately, it is also a hot bed for false prophets, false pastors, false apostles, and imposters of the gospel who are only in it to enrich themselves and their families. Many pastors are using witchcraft and powers of the marine kingdom (supernatural powers used underwater in the oceans of the earth) to attract people who have not studied the Word of God and gained understanding, which was also predicted to happen just before the Messiah returns.

It is written: "For false Christs and false prophets will appear and they will provide great signs and wonders, so as to deceive, if possible, even the elect (God's chosen ones)" (Mt 24:24 AMP).

It is written: "And many False prophets shall rise, and shall deceive many. And because iniquity shall abound, the love of many shall wax cold" (Mt 24:11-12 KJV).

In other words, false prophets shall go about deceiving people all over the world, and open sin and lawlessness will make many people become unloving and intolerant. This means that people worldwide will be less likely to forgive and give people second chances.

160

The African continent along with the Philippines in Asia also faces militant Muslim extremists. In Nigeria, Chad, Niger, and Cameroon, the authorities have to deal with Boko Haram, the Islamic terrorist group that engages in grotesque violence, and the Fulani Herdsmen. In East Africa, the Somalia-based terrorist organization called AlShabaab, which has ties to Al-Qaeda, has caused considerable trouble in relatively peaceful Kenya. Militant Muslim extremists are killing, raping, and maiming Christians from Nigeria, Central America, and Kenya. None of the Christian population is fighting back. Christians are choosing to rely on their governments to tackle the insurgency with the armed forces of these individual nations. More than 5,000 years ago, the Bible predicted that these dangerous, extreme Islamic elements would be a thorn in the flesh of all nations. They will be the descendants of Ishmael, the son of Abraham, who came from Sarah's maid Hagar.

It is written: "And the angel of the LORD said unto her, Behold, thou art with child and shalt bear a son, and shalt call his name Ishmael; because the LORD hath heard thy affliction. And he will be a wild man; his hand will be against every man, and every man's hand against him; and he shall dwell in the presence of al his brethren" (Gn 16:11-12 KJV).

Today, Islamic fundamentalists and their militant wings are in a global jihad, from Boko Haram in West and Central Africa to the Jihadist group in the Philippines, which is led by Abu Sayyaf.

These nations understand the U.S. Constitution and America's fight for independence. This is taught in world history in high schools. Many of these nations believe America's greatness is dependent on the country's relationship with God, not just on having a well-crafted constitution. They have seen how God has favored America like no other nation on Earth today. What made America and Western Europe rich was their faith in God and the covenant God had with their founding fathers. Yet this isn't the first time the Creator of heaven and Earth has intentionally favored one country over the other.

Nearly two centuries ago, there was an island nation known as Great Britain. It is still called that by those who relish the awesome power they had. But today, it is fair to say it is now referred to as the United Kingdom. So, what allowed a small island with no more than ten million people have so many colonies under its control? The gospel is the short answer. They always sent missionaries to minister the gospel to each territory they occupied, and sometimes they sent them before they occupied the place. They not only taught English, but they also built many Christians schools in which Bible study was part of the curriculum.

Many of the schools they built had a religious underpinning. The Methodist, Anglican, and Catholic churches in England built all manner of world-class high schools in their colonies, some that are still standing today. So God rewarded them by allowing them to have many territories all over the world. Great Britain was the largest empire in history between the 18th and 20th centuries. This is where the saying, "The sun never sets on the British Empire," came from, because while it was nighttime in Jamaica, it was sunny in Australia. And Great Britain owned both. The British had a strong navy, which helped propel them into being a formidable military power. That is why the United States has, as part of its defense strategy, the most powerful and most formidable blue water navy on Earth. We learned it from our former colonial master. Britain also owned Canada, India, Iraq, Nigeria, Egypt, South Africa, Kenya, and Barbados. Indeed, twothirds of the territories on Earth belonged to them. He who controls the seas rules the world. I say that the nation that spreads the gospel the most becomes the superpower.

Today, even though the Church is fading away in England, there is a spiritual battle waging to bring Great

162

Britain back to God. Efforts are being made, both behind the scene and with the knowledge of the powerful bishop of the Anglican Church, to get the gospel back to flourishing among its people. The battle for Britain has begun, and many African evangelists, and evangelists from other nations in the Caribbean and Asia, have been charged with the mantle of waking up the British people, showing them that will set them free to once more enjoy a special relationship with God. Unfortunately, the battle is hindered by the fact that many of the old churches of Britain have been converted into night clubs and mosques. Secularism is on the rise, and Islam is now one of the fastet growing religions in England.

The Imams of the Islamic faith have done a great job spreading their message to many curious British citizens. Unfortunately, the British authorities have one major problem, and I am not sure their security agencies are aware of it. Some of the immigrants do not really care about Great Britain. There are some people residing in England, particularly from the Islamic faith, who do not have the same patriotic mentality that immigrants in the U.S. have. They still see themselves as citizens of where they came from, and their allegiance to Britain is a distant second place. I would not be exaggerating in saying some of them do not even particularly like the British people, and this is sad because they are residing in their country. They are there for economic reasons, and they believe that one day they will take over the country and overrun Britain with their faith.

This is a sharp contrast from the United States, where immigrants are proud to identify with their new home and country. In fact, some legal residents in America love the country more than some of the people who were born here. Just recently, a friend of my wife's who was born here said she doesn't care much for the American flag and that it means nothing to her. This is not often the case for citizens of the United States who came into this country as immigrants. On occasion, when you run into a U.S. citizen who originally comes from somewhere like Azerbaijan, Nigeria, or Bangladesh and you ask them where they are originally from, they will look at you strangely and then tell you they are from somewhere like Lewisville, Rochester, Minnesota, or Palm Beach Florida. But then they laugh and tell you where they are originally from. There is such an instant sense of patriotism for America. Some of the legal immigrants in Britain are not aware of how God blessed Great Britain in the past and how the royal family of England knows and remembers this truth even though secularism is on the rise in England, and in most nations in Western Europe.

For example, there are still some strong, godly traditions that are practiced by the royal family in England. I was recently informed that when the royal family baptizes any of their newborn babies, they use water from the Jordan River to do it. According to Her Majesty Queen Elizabeth II, there is no exception to this rule among members of the royal family. Everyone must be baptized in the name of the Father, the Son, and the Holy Spirit. God save the queen, and God bless the queen.

In 1962, prayer was thrown out of our public schools by a landmark United States Supreme Court decision in which the court ruled it was unconstitutional for state officials to compose an official school prayer and encourage its recitation in public schools. Secondly, divorce began to grow among many secular and religious Christians. Then it exploded, even among the reborn Christians, in the 90s. As we entered the 21st century, people began to question the institution of marriage, as so many preachers of the gospel had become part of the divorce population. With all of this happening, it wasn't a surprise that calls began to be made for the redefinition of marriage in our laws. Many nations also began to follow the example of America as divorce increased in their respective countries.

164

At the same time, unknown to many Christians, the kingdom of darkness had released its global attack on the institution of marriage while the gospel was growing in the developing world, particularly in Africa. The developing nations were on fire for the things that pertained to God, and they celebrated the teachings of Jesus Christ. Leaders of nations with the fear of God were entering office either by democratic rule or by military coup. This came about at the time when many African countries were coming out of the long years of having a stagnant economy, droughts, poverty, Aids, and recession. It is important to point out that as the gospel was spreading in these nations, their economies began to grow. I remember being the special guest of the late President Nkurunziza of Burundi in September of 2011. I was part of a small team from Africa for Israel, and we were hoping to lobby for open relations with Israel. I can never forget the divine appointment we had. The president even opened the Bible to preach to us before we sat down for dinner. It is understood that in addition to his elite brigade of guards who protect him, he had a worship band made up of real soldiers who were part of his entourage when he traveled on vacation within Burundi. Burundi was one of the few countries that first volunteered troops to stabilize Somalia before the African Union raised a peacekeeping force there.

President George Bush—the 43rd president of the United States, who publicly declared he was reborn—spearheaded a world bank program that allowed the forgiveness of debt for many of these African nations. This was one of his greatest crown achievements in office, and it will be greatly rewarded in heaven. Many of these nations were riddled with debt and had little or no money to put into much-needed infrastructure. They needed hospitals, schools, the availability of water, and the rebuilding of new electrical grids in order to replace the ones that had been there since these nations were under colonial rule. As soon as their debt was wiped out, their economies began to grow, as they could channel vital resources to the things they needed.

During this period, President Obama's economic policy had a greater emphasis on trade with the emerging economies in Asia rather than in Africa. In recent years, before Covid-19, African nations have been some of the fastest developing countries in the world, recording a higher growth rate than some of the developed nations. Unfortunately for the U.S., our leaders did not seize the opportunity in front of them, so China then swooped into Africa and made billions and billions of dollars in trade profits. They engaged in barter trade and won rights to many African nations' natural resources. These African nations would have preferred to have worked with the United States. I am not sure what President Obama's strategy was in regard to Africa. Some of their trade practices with China have left much to be desired. Nevertheless, China has major capital projects in all fifty-four nations in Africa.

W was the nickname for President Bush, and he embarked on an amazing project worthy of recognition. He should have been given a Nobel Peace Prize for this gracious policy. He brought the private sector of the pharmaceutical industry together in partnership with the United States in order to solve the Aids pandemic in Africa, which had already taken so many lives. Today, in Africa, people with this disease can now live normal lives thanks to President Bush. Those of us who are reborn believe God used him to reward Africa for drawing closer to Elohim Chayim. President Bush continues to quietly support other projects in Africa. May the Almighty God grant him a long life for endeavoring to preserve the lives of others. May God's goodness and mercies follow Bush all the days of his life.

As the nations of the world turned, it came as no surprise that African nations and the Christian community in Asia, Central America, South America, and Australia were completely caught off guard when a landmark ruling by the Supreme Court of the United States legalized same sex marriage on June 26, 2015. It stunned the African nations that had been celebrating the gospel that had been taught to them by the American pastors, prophets, and evangelists during huge rallies for more three decades. These nations admired and looked up to the United States. They were flabbergasted but, at the same time, felt that it was inevitable in America, as the LGBTQ community had been gaining a lot of clout in recent years.

These nations were concerned about what was taking place in America, but they did not seem too bothered about it until President Obama began playing the role of spokesman for the LGBTQ during his visits around the world. After that, nearly all of the African nations began passing laws in the opposite direction in regard to gay marriage. They stiffened the penalty, sometimes almost unfairly, for being part of the LGBTQ group in their respective countries. In fact, in the beginning, persecution of the LGBTQ began to grow in these countries, but later there were some much-needed reforms. They were also encouraged by the division in the U.S. over this Supreme Court ruling.

At first these countries had been happy about America having her first black leader. They understood that President Barack Obama had been put in office by God because of the death of Abraham Lincoln, who was assassinated and paid the ultimate price for his fearless role in fighting for freedom for blacks. They felt that God had chosen someone very similar to Lincoln—they were both tall, they both had ears that stuck out, and they both ran for Congress and lost. Ironically, when President Obama was asked which previous leader he admired the most, he chose Abraham Lincoln, who was a Republican. I remember that it caused some concern among Democrats because he did not choose a former Democratic leader. After Obama's actions regarding the LGBTQ, however, African nations were no longer sure where President Obama stood in spiritual matters. A big issue was that Obama didn't seem to really believe in his heart that it was the grace of God that put him in the White House. Did President Obama believe that the one who said, "Vengeance *is* mine; I will repay" (Rom 12:19 KJV), was the one who got him into office? It is a good question to ask him, as what unfolded in his second term left much to be desired.

Many reborn Christians believe President Obama thinks his calm demeanor, oratorical skills, the discipline he brings to the table when doing interviews, his aura, and his personal charisma are what got him into the White House. He also had David Axelrod, a brilliant campaign consultant, who helped guide and propel him to office. There is no question that this is true in the physical, but the decision was made in heaven to allow him to win because God was not interested in the alternatives. For example, God moved in the heart of the lion of the Senate, the late Senator Ted Kennedy, and told him to endorse President Obama instead of Hillary Clinton. This was a major game changer, and it moved other Democratic Senators, whose states Hillary won, to still endorse Obama. Without the Kennedy endorsement, Hillary would have won the democratic primaries, and she would have come into to power as the first female president of America in 2008.

Therefore, let it be known today that the sovereign will of God allowed the late Ted Kennedy, like him or hate him, to survive the Chappaquiddick scandal that began in July of 1969, which most ordinary Americans would be in jail for. He was protected so he could do what he did for President Obama, and after this accomplishment he died of brain cancer. The mindset of heaven is leaps and bounds ahead of the mortal man on Earth. And yet we think we are wiser than God, and we try to change how marriage is meant to be. Joseph, the famous Hebrew son of Jacob, had to be sold into slavery if he was to become the vice president of ancient Egypt. Remember, his oldest brother, Reuben, wanted to save him from the murderous and jealous spirit that was in his brothers, but he was sold into slavery before this could happen. Had Reuben succeeded in returning Joseph to his father, Joseph would not have become the most powerful leader on Earth in the time of his reign in Egypt. Again, God's ways are so different from man's. The Bible informs us that God's thoughts are not our thoughts

It is written: "Do you see someone skilled in their work? They will serve before kings; they will not serve before officials of low rank" (Prv 22:29 NIV).

The press could not get enough of President Obama; they adored him. I never met President Obama in person, but I did see him at a rally at the Target Center in Minneapolis in 2009, when he wasn't sure his cherished healthcare bill would pass. The first time I set my eyes on him was in a vision in January of 2007, when God informed me clearly that he would become the next president of the United States. The vision is still very vivid, and I saw how the press would elevate him and help him. I kept asking God, "What about Hillary," but He never answered me. Today, I stand with those whom God stands with, regardless of their political party.

The rise of President Trump to presidency in the United States of America was hidden from all but a few people. The media were completely caught off guard, with the exception of Dick Morris, the former campaign manager of Bill Clinton in his re-election. Dick Morris kept saying on television that Trump was going to win, but few would listen. The Trump presidency put an end to a massive plot to oppress the Christians in America, which would have had a worldwide ripple effect. Trump's rise to office also delayed the beginning of the end times. Had he lost the election in 2016, things would be very different. He has become a thorn in the flesh of those who want to institute the one world order. As Christians we know this is inevitable because Scriptures cannot be broken or unraveled. That said, we can buy time to win more souls for the Kingdom of God.

Decisions made in the Supreme Court have major spiritual ramifications, and the ruling by the U.S. Supreme Court on the gay marriage issue was no different. It woke up the consciousness of many Christians, including people who considered themselves passive Christians or Christians who only celebrated Easter and Christmas, rarely stepping into a church. There is no question that President Obama caved in to the enormous pressure put on him by the highly organized and powerful gay and lesbian lobby in Congress. They had helped him win his re-election bid in 2012, and now it was payback time. The problem was that President Obama never really realized that God had given him two terms already, and so he did not need to support a policy that would have strong spiritual repercussions. America had enjoyed special protections from God, and these protections were not guaranteed forever. It was clear he was unfamiliar with the things of the spiritual realm. To be fair, he is a constitutional lawyer and scholar. He did not go to the Supreme Court to challenge the Christians who were opposed to amending the long-standing marriage laws in the United States. He simply asked his justice department not to fight it. Let it be known that in his race for presidency, President Obama did not originally support gay marriage, but then he felt he needed the gay community to win the re-election.

I don't know how the LGBTQ felt about being used by Obama. They probably did not care, because they got the quid pro quo of maximum support for their goal to get gay marriage legalized. The LGBTQ are a highly sophisticated group of Americans. They are educated, smart, driven, and, above all, highly organized. I have friends in this community, and I stood with them many times in the late 80s and early 90s, when they did not have the clout that they have today. I stood with them when they were severely persecuted for just being gay. Yet at no time was I in agreement about amending the marriage laws to include gay marriage, because God is opposed to it, period.

Contrary to the false narrative, many Christians have friends in the gay community. We are called to love one another by Jesus Christ Himself, for heaven's sake. We are not called to agree with each other's personal lifestyles or political philosophies. The Christians were opposed to gay marriage for all the right reasons, the foremost being the fear of God, because they knew what this would do to our country spiritually, and they knew about the doors it would open to Satan. To the gays and lesbians, it was marriage equality. To the Christians it was disobedience to the powerful God of heaven and Earth. They could care less if some people in the Jewish community in America—including those in the corridors of power in Washington, who should have known better, given their history and how their God has acted in the past—chose out of their own volition to betray Hashem on this divisive issue.

The LGBTQ had built a successful movement and spread their tentacles to all levels of the government long before the decision to legalize gay marriage had reached the Supreme Court. They framed their message in two words: Marriage Equality. Make sure you do your homework before you take on this formidable group. Nevertheless, the Word of God will stand forever, and all other things you see today, including the LGBTQ, will pass away. God created marriage, not man. So it is God who sets the principles and guidelines on how this institution must function. Now, let me be frank with Christians. It is indeed difficult to fight another group of people asking for an expansion in the definition of marriage when many of the Christians have made a mockery of marriage themselves with their high divorce rates. Nevertheless, in the eyes of God and man, two wrongs do not make anything right.

God loves the gays and lesbians, but God would never contradict Himself to satisfy any group of people.

We are the ones who have to conform to His will and enter into repentance for our sins rather than celebrate them. Nevertheless, I believe the recent ruling by the Supreme Court, which outlawed any form of discrimination against gays and lesbians in the workplace, was a victory not just this group but for all Americans. God's disagreement with an alternative form of marriage is not a license to discriminate against them in the workplace, as long as it doesn't force religious institutions to hire members from this community against their will. It is also ironic that the judge who gave the sweeping victory to the highly organized gay and lesbian community was Neil Gorsuch, who was appointed by none other than President Donald J. Trump. Trump had been vindicated in his quest to appoint judges who strictly interpreted the Constitution.

God loves America despite her faults and some of the choices Americans have made. We are still His favorite children because we have helped to spread the gospel to the whole world. Yes, Israel is His baby, but Israelites haven't, in modern times, spread the gospel like America has, with the exception of when the Church was born in Antioch right after the Pentecost. Nevertheless, as it is prophesized in the Bible, the chosen Jews will be the main evangelists during the end times, and in the time of the great tribulation. Their time has not yet come, despite the preaching of the gospel by the Messianic Jews today. Their preaching is a sign that that time draws near. The Bible is indeed a very powerful book of prophecy. How can you be a politician in Washington today and not read it? Do you think that you are wiser than God?

God raised up Donald J. Trump, someone with no political experience, except that he previously supported candidates from both parties in order to keep his influence in Washington D.C. as a businessman. Therefore, it wasn't a surprise when it came out that Trump supported Hillary Clinton financially, regardless of the amount. He gave to her campaign in her race to represent New York in the Senate. God chose Donald Trump for a completely different reason from why he allowed President Obama to become the 44th president of the United States. God is sovereign. God is not a Republican or a Democrat, even though he rode a donkey (Democratic symbol) to Jerusalem. He did not ride into Jerusalem with a big elephant from India. So, Republicans, do not think you own the presidency. He will put whoever He wants there. It is all based on His sovereign will. God got involved to ensure that President Obama did not inherit a successor, and He wiped out literally everything in terms of the major policies Obama passed through executive orders. You see, God always has His way because He is sovereign and very powerful. The only exception was the healthcare plan known as Obama Care, which was passed thanks to former Senator Al Franken. There is a strong, spiritual reason why all efforts by the Republicans to remove Obamacare have failed. I would rather speak about this truth than write about it in this book, but it will be an eye-opener, even for President Obama, and his fear of God will grow after that. Therefore, Obamacare can only be improved upon rather than being completely erased.

The prophetic Word had gone out about Trump's presidency years before he came to power by the retired fire fighter Mark Taylor, who is a reborn Christian. God speaks to the reborn through the Holy Spirit rather than to people who go to church but are not reborn. He did not speak first with the pastors of the biggest churches; He spoke to His chosen few, the shepherds watching their flock, as it was when Jesus was born. Weren't any Democrats aware of this? It is even on YouTube. President Trump was put in power by God. Nobody could have defeated the Clinton machine except God, and this was true with Obama and Trump in 2016.

Christians must understand—and I know they do—that prophecy and knowledge do not guarantee you anything if

173

you do not take the corresponding action on Earth through prayer and fasting in order to birth the prophecy into the earth. For not all prophecy that is revealed, even coming from genuine prophets, comes to pass. God has the final say, and He demonstrated through the prophet Samuel, who anointed both King Saul and King David. In other words, God can change His mind on a prophecy His servants on the earth have made. There is still a chance it will not come to pass even though all genuine prophecy is inspired by the Holy Spirit. He rarely does this, though, because God knows it would discredit His prophets. God made sure everything Samuel said came to pass, which means God brought it to pass because He loved and trusted Samuel.

It is written: "The LORD was with Samuel as he grew up, and he let none of Samuel's words fall to the ground. And all Israel from Dan to Beersheba recognized that Samuel was attested as a prophet of the LORD" (1 Sm 3:19-20 NIV).

Another sign that Trump's victory in 2016 was God's will was the fact that the main press, including CNN and John King, missed it so badly when it came to deciding who was likely to win. President Trump, as we all know now, was also surprised by his upset victory and did not believe the mighty men of God who had told him nine months before the election that he was going to be the next president. So how on earth could he have colluded with Russia? You see, you would have to be gullible and naïve to believe this false narrative that has unfortunately divided the nation, families, friends, and even churches. God has judged the main press for their role in dividing this country because their preferred candidate did not win. The judgment is severe, and it has been coming slowly. God's hope is that they will repent before it is fully unleashed.

When God makes a decision about Earth, the physical manifestation of this decision may not make sense to most people. Most people in the world are unaware of the season we are in and how things are going to be black and white.

174

God is anything but a people pleaser. The people of the world tell us they do not want religious morality forced on them. But as Pastor Jeffress of Dallas Baptist Church said, "If we acquiesce to their demands, then their agenda is what gets put in place, which is not the agenda of God." There are two opposing groups, and each side has a right to fight for its own agenda. But don't hate the people who win, especially in a democracy. Jesus accurately predicted that many would not be able to discern the season we are in. It's just as it was in the past, when the Pharisees and Sadducees of Israel did not even know the Messiah was in their midst even though they had studied about Him for years. It is written: "Now The Pharisees and Sadducees came up, and testing Jesus [to get something to use against Him], they asked Him to show them a sign from heaven [which would support His divine authority]. But He replied to them, 'When it is evening, you say, "It *will be* fair weather, for the sky is red." And in the morning, "It *will be* stormy today, for the sky is red and has a threatening look." You know how to interpret the appearance of the sky, but cannot interpret the signs of the times?'" (Mt 16:1-3 AMP).

Today, we are experts in doing exactly that. We can spot a hurricane descending on Florida or the Caribbean nations hundreds of miles away, and we can even measure the intensity of the hurricane, but we are unable to discern the things of the Spirit as it relates to our dear nation.

When God wants to do something major in any nation, He speaks to His people first, as He did with Abraham, so nothing has changed under the sun since then. He reveals to His prophets first, and then he reveals to the pastors who are deep in the things of God—the ones who are often praying for the country and every president, regardless of whether they voted for them or not. He has his handpicked intercessors on the earth who are praying and fasting for long periods of time. He gives them insight and shares dreams with them about things concerning the nations of the world. Sometimes the prophets don't always agree with God's decision and are in denial. For example, the Obama election and re-election. God is not concerned about the flesh's response as long as His will is done.

It is written: "For God speaketh once, yea twice, yet man perceiveth it not. In a dream, in a vision of the night, when deep sleep falleth upon men, in slumberings upon the bed; Then he openeth the ears of men, and sealeth their instruction, That he may withdraw man from his purpose, and hide pride from man. He keepeth back his soul from the pit, and his life from perishing by the sword" (Jb 33:14-18 KJV).

Ironically, every race and ethnic group, including reborn blacks in the United States, that did not support the Supreme Court ruling legalizing gay marriage had voted for President Trump. The main press have hidden the truth from the American people about why Trump won. But not for long. It is being exposed now. Maybe the press had this information but chose to give a different reason and push a false narrative. That is why, my brothers and sisters, Trump had an unusual number of black votes for a guy the press had told us, without any compelling evidence, was a bigot, homophobic, misogynist, and anything else they could say to discredit his rise to power. The hand of God denied Obama a successor, and there is nothing Hillary Clinton could have done to turn it around. I was made aware of Trump becoming president by the Spirit of God nearly three months before the election, and I informed my wife in early October. I was also informed in my heart that God was going to deal with the press. There was no point praying for Hillary, as judgment had been made in Heaven. She should run again after Trump's second term and put her faith in God rather than man. It is written: "...Thy will be done in earth, as it is heaven" (Mt 6:10 KJV).

Trump also got support from many who considered themselves libertarians; they were not opposed to gay

176

marriage as long as it was approved through state or federal legislation or by a referendum, but they loathed the legislating from the bench by the Supreme Court. The LGBTQ will argue that if they went through that channel, they wouldn't have the victory they got at the Supreme Court, and they are right about that. The libertarians were afraid of the precedent it would set. Many who were intimidated by the gay and lesbian lobby did not openly express their opposition, lest they be called bigots or ran out of business if they owned one. They all cast their votes quietly for President Trump. That is how he won. According to the media, though, he got into power because of the support he received from the white majority, the far right, the religious, and people who have "no common sense." In other words, the undesirables. Oh, and let's not forget Russia. But nothing could be further from the truth. Americans are smart people; they know the media lies because they know what they cast on their ballots in 2016. Thank God for the secret ballot in America.

Putting faith and religion aside, how could the Democrats not see the handwriting on the wall? It was all over the map in the United States. California is a state that hasn't voted for a Republican president since the time of Ronald Reagan in 1984. This is because the state is the home base of the Hollywood actors and actresses who are sympathetic to the Democratic party. Besides, California is the bedroom of liberals. When California had a referendum on the ballot on whether to ban gay marriages in 2008, it actually passed, to the unpleasant surprise of the LGBTQ community. The Democratic party should have taken notice and recognized that the religious allegiance on this issue was still very potent, and it transcended political parties. This also happened at the time when the state voted overwhelmingly for President Barack Obama.

This referendum passed despite San Francisco being the nerve center of the gay community. This should have been a red flag to the Democrats to tread with caution on this issue.

On the other hand, what it did do was galvanize the LGBTQ lobby and deepen their resolve to develop a new strategy to get their agenda of marriage equality through. However, many in this community overplayed their hand in their quest to legalize gay marriage. Many who have friends from that community but do not support gay marriage were wrongly labeled as bigots, and they were accused of being filled with the spirit of intolerance. Some of the people who voted to ban gay marriage in that 2008 referendum were ostracized and even poorly treated by a few extreme members of that group.

The more you characterize people as bigots because of where they stand on this divisive issue, the more it undermines the cause of the LGBTQ. These individuals took their stance because they feared God, and they knew the end times were drawing near. As I said earlier on, I supported gay rights in the late 80s, when there were hardly any Democrats behind them. I felt love was the best way to reach out to them, not persecution or discrimination. Christ calls us to love one another but to reject the sins of one another. I just never allowed my support to get to the point of supporting the overturning of the marriage laws God instituted.

Some good things have come out of the lobby efforts of that community, and I applaud them.

Many emerging and developing nations instituted reforms to allow for LGBTQ rights, but these same nations drew a line when it came to gay marriages. For example, out of fifty-four African countries, only two countries have marriage laws like the United States and Western Europe, and those are Cape Verde and South Africa. Most nations in the developing world—particularly in Africa, Asia, and South America—have resisted pressure from the United States to expand the definition of marriage beyond what was clearly prescribed by God. In a nutshell, the African nations were not diplomatic at all when they let former President

178

Obama know they were not interested in emulating the America's approval of gay marriage. They strongly believed what was taking place in America, known in Nigeria as God's country, was indeed the sign of the coming of the end times. It is written: "The fear of the LORD is the beginning of wisdom…" (Prv 9:10 KJV). African nations' reverence and fear of the Lord fortified their decision not to tamper with their existing marriage laws. In other words, they were not afraid of former President Obama; they were afraid of God.

It is written: "For [God does not overlook sin and] the wrath of God is revealed from heaven against all ungodliness and unrighteousness of men who in their wickedness suppress *and* stifle the truth, because that which is known about God is evident within them [in their inner consciousness], for God made it evident to them. For ever since the creation of the world His invisible attributes, His eternal power and divine nature, have been clearly seen, being understood through His workmanship [all His creation, the wonderful things that He has made], so that they [who fail to believe and trust in Him] are without excuse *and* without defense" (Rom 1:18-20 AMP).

One of the increasingly successful ways atheists and people on the far left legitimize their activities is by discrediting the existence of a heaven and hell. They know they cannot deny that there was an incredible Savior of the world, who came to redeem mankind. There would be a global uproar if they did that, so they now go to great lengths to misrepresent what He says. When they water down the reality of rewards and punishments after death, it becomes very easy for society to accept anything with little or no resistance. Remember, if you stand for nothing, you will fall for everything. A society without boundaries eventually breads a lawless generation. Nevertheless, to say that President Obama did not have any impact at all would be a mistake. Many of the African nations have relaxed their laws pertaining to the LGBTQ. The killing and torturing of gays and lesbians, which even Jesus Christ Himself would have vehemently disapproved of and condemned, has gone down considerably, and this is great news. All Christians must fight against the killing, persecution, and torture of any member of the LGBTQ in other countries. Persecution continues, but even in Lagos, Nigeria, which is the New York of Africa, gays and lesbians are gaining acceptance. This is important because Nigeria is the most religious nation on Earth, evenly divided between the Muslims and Christians. As long as Nigeria continues not recognizing gay marriage, no African nations will either. They still look up to Nigeria as the giant of Africa despite its shortcomings. Nigeria and the United States are inextricably tied together in the realm of the spirits. Today, there are many churches pastored by Nigerians in the United States. Most of these churches have had their issues and setbacks, but they have two things in common: the fear of the Lord and the full understanding of the seasons and times we are in.

South Africa is one of the two nations that voted to allow gay marriage in Africa. This country has the highest number of reported rapes in Africa, and the high number of unresolved cases of rape made the country more subservient to pressure from the Western nations. That is why it was easy to pass a law in that nation to legalize gay marriage. God oversees nations. With all the challenges Nigeria faces, including the battles with Boko Haram and not even having a constant source of electricity, it still overtook South Africa as the largest economy in Africa in 2014. Keep in mind that Nigeria overtook the South African economy even though South Africa is far more advanced than Nigeria in many ways. In fact, many Nigerian citizens have moved to South Africa for work and a better quality of life. Discrimination today is rift between Nigerians and South Africans, and innocent people have been killed.

If President Obama noticed, he accomplished more in his first term than he did in his second term, and it was spiritual. President Obama never figured out that God's will is always done. In his first term President Obama stabilized the U.S. economy after the severe 2008 recession, and he made progress with his service chiefs and security team in preventing certain terrorist attacks on the United States. He used drone strikes, with maximum efficiency, to take out the enemies of America. He was responsible for having a Navy Seal team kill Bin Laden. When he strayed from the things of God and began to celebrate sin by allowing the lights of the LGBTQ flag reflect on the White House, he was done. The man I had championed and taken the heat for supporting had fallen from grace. He couldn't keep his promise to reign in Syria following their use of chemical weapons and their atrocities in the civil war. To be fair, it may be because he wasn't sure who used chemical weapons: the opposition or the Assad regime. Then Russians invaded Ukraine in 2014, and he couldn't really do much but put some out sanctions, which only emboldened Russia under Putin to get more aggressive in Syria and usurp the United States authority in the Middle East. Then the civil war in Libya broke out, and it was a disaster even though Gadhafi was successfully overthrown and eventually killed.

President Obama had no idea it is God who makes presidents successful. Not even Senator McConnell of Kentucky could block President Obama's appointed judges if God wanted them on the bench. I believe judges that adhere to the strict interpretation of the Constitution are important to God regardless of their political party, as the Constitution was inspired by the Word of God. Yet the worst was yet to come. God was going to deny President Obama a successor regardless of who was running for president, especially if their policies were to remain unchanged or move in a trajectory God wasn't pleased with. Some of the founding fathers of this nation who were reborn, and past presidents who have gone on to heaven, were restraining God's judgment on America, and Trump was the break they needed. Otherwise, America, just like Israel in the past, would have faced dire consequences because Satan, the accuser of brethren, would have been pointing to God. And God, being a just God, would have to act by bringing judgement upon America.

We know God hates injustice against the poor and oppression of the less fortunate. God hates it when we misuse the earth's resources and make life more unhabitable for the next generation. There are plenty of stories in the Bible about Jesus' disdain for people who did not manage what was given to them properly. We are the only people created in His own image; He did not send His only begotten Son to die for aliens in Mars or Jupiter. So He comes down very strong on state-sponsored and state-sanctioned sexual immorality. The Bible gives us a clear picture of how God handles these two different situations. They are not the same. On one hand, God would use His power like He did in Egypt during the time of Moses, when He made sure the Israelites who were enslaved by Egyptians were vindicated and paid back in full for lost wages. This is how He deals with injustice and discrimination against the poor or ethnic minorities. God allowed one of the greatest wealth transfers in history to take place by taking from the rich and giving to the poor. God plundered the Egyptian task masters who had greatly oppressed the Israelites. God supernaturally told the Egyptians to literally give all their gold and high-priced jewels to the Israelites. The net worth of that would be in the billions today. It was payback time for God for His people, the Israelites. When the Egyptians realized what they had just done, they decided to go after the Israelites who had departed from Egypt. El-Gibhor, the mighty God of Israel, protected the Israelites by drowning the most elite Egyptian soldiers in the Red Sea. This is how He deals with economic injustice against the poor. But when it comes to sexual immorality, God can destroy a whole city if it becomes so rampant, or He can destroy the whole world, as He did during Noah's time. He will only do this when sin is celebrated rather than repented for, when vile and degrading things are done to the innocent, when children's lives are destroyed. Adults can do what they want, within the law, but to travel to places like Thailand and the Dominican Republic in order to have sex with minors is offensive to God. He destroyed the world during Noah's time because fallen angels from the kingdom of Satan had entered into the daughters of the world and perverted the seed of God, raising giants. So, in His burning anger He destroyed the world with water. Everyone knows the story about Sodom and Gomorrah. Most people do not know that God actually wanted to spare Sodom and Gomorrah from impending destruction. He was so merciful that He sent two intelligence-gathering angels from heaven to find out if what they were hearing about the wickedness in Sodom and Gomorrah was true. God knew it was true. He is all-knowing. But He still sent those angels just in case He was missing something or the report had some errors. When the angels went there, it was worse than they thought, and the people there wanted to have sex with the angels. This was enough, and God sent burning Sulphur on that city. Now, no one in their right mind dared to call God a bigot, or homophobic, or unprogressive. The one who decides who survives a pandemic and who doesn't is still in charge of the world. I tell you this, lest we all be deceived that we are in control.

It is God who lifts one nation up and brings another down. He is the sovereign ruler of the heavens and Earth, even in a democracy. Know this today: No president of the United States has risen into the office and occupied the White House without the prior knowledge and approval of God. Listen to what the prophet Daniel—a Hebrew young man who came from the royal family of Israel and was exiled to Babylon after the king of Babylon invaded Israel and successfully conquered them because of their disobedience to God—said.

It is written: "'Praise be to the name of God for ever and ever; wisdom and power are his. He changes times and seasons; he deposes kings and raises up others. He gives wisdom to the wise and knowledge to the discerning. He reveals deep and hidden things; he knows what lies in darkness, and light dwells with him. I thank and praise you, God of my ancestors: You have given me wisdom and power, you have made known to me what we asked of you, you have made known to us the dream of the king'" (Dn 2:20-23 Bible).

Daniel's story is legendary, true, factual, and not subject to debate. There was a powerful leader in ancient Babylon called King Nebuchadnezzar. He had a dream that deeply troubled him, and none of his magicians and dream interpreters could interpret the dream. Their gods were powerless to tell the king about his dream, let alone interpret it. Now, it goes without saying that the king was frustrated and angry because none of his wise men or magicians could tell him about the dream he had. For man this is impossible. So, in his frustration and anger, the king ordered all the wise men in the land executed. This means that Daniel, who was unaware of what was going on, had to be included because he was known to operate using the wisdom of God to solve problems. When Arioch, the captain of the king's bodyguard, went to look for Daniel in order to carry out the king's order, Daniel used wisdom and discretion to find out from Arioch why the king was been so harsh and angry. Arioch then relayed the entire matter to Daniel. Daniel went to the king and asked for twenty-four hours to tell him about his dream and then interpret the dream for him. When you think about it, this was insane, an impossible mission. But with God all things are possible (Lk 1:37). Daniel conferred with his close-knit group of God-fearing men (Hanniah, Mishael, and Azariah), and after they had sought the Lord in prayer, He revealed the king's dream and gave the interpretation to Daniel. Daniel thanked the God of heaven and Earth with the above-mentioned prayer. Daniel was then promoted to be either vice president or prime minister after he successfully told King Nebuchadnezzar the dream and meaning.

According to historical accounts, more than 3,000 years ago, when King Cyrus invaded Persia, he did so in a surprise invasion at night by using a tunnel that took them right into the heart of Babylon. Daniel, who was still in Babylon and had served under King Nebuchadnezzar, gave King Cyrus a scroll that told exactly what he had just accomplished in his invasion. It even said in the scroll when and what time King Cyrus would become king according to the prophet Jeremiah. This blew the mind of King Cyrus, and from that day, even though he neither worshiped or prayed to the God of the Hebrews, he feared the God of Abraham, Isaac, and Israel and quickly caught up on the things that pertain to the powerful God of heaven and Earth. To say the least, Cyrus liked Daniel and promoted him to a high office in his administration.

It is written: "'This is what Cyrus king of Persia says: "The LORD, the God of heaven, has given me all the kingdoms of the earth and he has appointed me to build a temple for him at Jerusalem in Judah. Any of his people among you may go up to Jerusalem in Judah and build the temple of the LORD, the God of Israel, the God who is in Jerusalem, and may their God be with them. And in any locality where survivors may now be living, the people are to provide them with silver and gold, with goods and livestock, and with freewill offerings for the temple of god in Jerusalem"'" (Ezr 1:2-4 NIV).

It is also understood that after issuing a decree allowing the exiled Jews to return back to their homeland, King Cyrus also ordered all the precious metals and articles—which had been catered away by King Nebuchadnezzar of

185

Babylon and brought to his empire—to be returned back to Jerusalem and placed in the temple that was going to be built. He ordered Mithredath, his all-powerful treasurer of the empire, to see to it that the gold, silver, and other articles were returned back to the temple in Jerusalem.

Isaiah also prophesied about King Cyrus being a person who would overcome his adversaries because God's hand was on him even though he did not know God (worship Him).

It is written: "'This is what the LORD says to his anointed, to Cyrus, whose right hand I take hold of to subdue nations before him and to strip kings of their armor, to open doors before him so that gates will not be shut: I will go before you and will level the mountains; I will break down gates of bronze and cut through bars of iron. I will give you hidden treasures, riches stored in secret places, so that you may know I am the LORD..." (Is 45:1-3 NIV).

It is written: "I will raise up Cyrus in my righteousness: I will make all his ways straight. He will rebuild my city and set my exiles free, but not for a price or reward, says the LORD Almighty" (Is 45:13 NIV).

Cyrus is mentioned around twenty-three times in the Old Testament. Those of you who are atheists are missing out big time, because the Bible is also a historical book. What is interesting is that Cyrus did not know the God of Abraham, Isaac, and Israel. He was a pagan, but God raised him up to allow the Israelites to return to Israel after being released from their captivity in the Persian Empire, which had control over Babylon, where the Jews were residing for disobeying God. I hope all Americans are listening. God is still in charge despite the outbreak of the Coronavirus. King Cyrus granted the Jews safe passage back home, and he allowed them to return to their land and rebuild Jerusalem and its temple. All of these actions were the fulfillment of prophecy written in in 2 Chronicles 36, 22, and 23, and in the first chapter of the book of Ezra.

186

So, listen to me, Democrats, Republicans, Independents, and Socialists: God hasn't changed at all. He still acts in the affairs of nations when it is in the strategic interest of His Kingdom. God's purpose always trumps what happens in the physical. He has the power to cause mankind to vote in a certain way in a democracy. It also underscores the absolute greatness of the Bible that a prophecy about an incoming king of a foreign nation was made before the king was born. Which intelligence agency can match this kind of excellent prediction? The short answer is NONE!

Before President Clinton came to power, the late President George Bush had just won the Persian Gulf War, and he had a 92% approval rating. He was poised for re-election, but God's eyes were on a young man who was developing a strong friendship with Israel and whose humble background pleased God. He came from Little Rock, Arkansas. He wasn't perfect, and sin was after him from the beginning. God knew that. He was a gifted orator. In the beginning he showed signs of knowledge of the Word of God, even though he shared his approval of gay marriages in a rare interview with Anderson Cooper after he left office. I am not sure why he said the things he said in that interview. He wrongly thought it would help his wife's quest for the presidency. That was a mistake.

Nevertheless, Clinton grew up in the Baptist Church, and he knew that segregation was wrong. This alone pleased God. When President Clinton came to power, our country was in a recession, and we had a huge trade deficit with one of our trading partners in Asia, just like we have today with China. The nation we had the deficit with then was Japan. The trade deficit was crushing our economy from the late 80s to the early 90s. Then President Clinton among many other notable things he did, including cooperating with the republicans on the hill when Newt Gingrich was the Speaker and came to power with a bold mandate called 'The Contract For America' also hired an astute California

Lawyer Mickey Cantor as the U.S. trade representative. Clinton then tapped Cantor to renegotiate trade with Japan, who was our largest trading partner at that time. The result was twenty-two million jobs created during his two terms in office. He put a 100,000 police officers on the street. He lowered the crime rate to the lowest it had been in thirty years. He ended the Kosovo and Balkan War by ordering Major General Wesley Clark to bomb Serbia for forty days. He then embarked on shuttle diplomacy, using the late Richard Holbroke to broker a peace deal in Dayton, Ohio.

He nearly solved the Middle East crisis permanently at the Y River Accord with Madelene Albright, a veteran diplomat and the first female Secretary of State. Thank God he did not, because the Bible says only the antichrist will do this, and it will only last three-and-a-half years before it will fall apart. I should mention this: Some Christians were watching to see whether he was the antichrist, and this is bizarre and somewhat funny. I never thought he was. And finally, Bill Clinton brought the deficit to zero and said that if we continued using his policy, we would eventually wipe out the then two trillion-dollar debt in a matter of years. His sins were forgiven, but God denied him a successor because he had desecrated the oval office with his sin. Yet God, in His mercy, blocked his removal from office after his impeachment by causing some Republicans to vote in his favor. I was one of the many praying that he wouldn't be removed from office, although I was also praying the sin wouldn't be belittled, as some Democrats tend to do. Sin is sin in the eyes of God, but God is faithful, and His mercies endure forever. What is ironic is that some of the Republicans who were accusing President Clinton of indiscretion also fell from the same sin within a year. He left office with a high approval rating.

President Trump has had an uphill battle from the start of his administration. The main press have adamantly opposed him in every way. Prior to 2016, America had a vibrant independent press, but now the media heavily support the Democratic party. I have never seen anything like this in my nearly forty years in the United States, and it is insane. The media were very upset that their candidate of choice, Hillary Clinton, lost the election. They declared war against Trump, and he, in return, gave them a label that has become famous: Fake News! Millions of Americans believe that if Ted Turner still owned CNN, he would not have joined forces with other news channels to make life extremely difficult for President Trump. I remember when CNN had Bernard Shaw, Alicia Wallace, and Lou Dobbs. Then, CNN was at its best. It is really so sad to see what the media have become today, as compared to the glory days, when Anderson Cooper was a veteran wartime correspondent covering the war in the Balkans under very dangerous and difficult conditions. I often prayed for his safety.

Today, the battle wages on till November of 2020. Yet I will tell you the truth, just as I told the truth about Obama to the reborn church in early 2007: Trump was chosen by God for reasons totally different from what most people would think. Trump was chosen because he is not polished; he is rough around the edges. He's not a smooth-talking politician; he is plainspoken. Above all, he is the polar opposite of President Obama in every way. God knew he was going to do what was right for America, not what was politically expedient. He is not a typical Republican candidate; he is more Independent-minded. He understands the agenda the Chinese have for America. Some democratic leaders wouldn't admit it, but they were very okay with China eventually becoming the next economic superpower, as they felt it was their turn. Except for Senator Chuck Schumer of New York, who has appreciated the way Trump deals with China. Based on how quickly China notified the world about the virus from Wuhan, the whole world can now see what life would be like if China held that power. China is a great nation, and it has a rich history, but their handling of the spread of the Coronavirus greatly undermined their credibility in the eyes of the world.

Trump's growing support in the black community is a very terrible headache to the Democratic party, and they simply cannot understand how he does it. Just recently, President Trump, for all his many faults, once again demonstrated political brinksmanship by introducing a program that appears promising and encouraging for job seekers. Trump knew minorities and people without college degrees were left behind in the new global economy. He had a plan, and with Ivanka Trump, he signed an executive order that places more emphasis on one's work experience than having a college degree for jobs within the federal government. This bold initiative barely made it in the news. Another welcome policy has been the release of nonviolent offenders from prison; most were incarcerated for being caught during the "three strikes and you're out" rule that was introduced during the Reagan and Clinton administrations. Yes, Trump's mannerism leaves much to be desired sometimes, but he was not hired to be a well-mannered president; he was elected to get the job done and make America great again.

God wanted to glorify His name by using a nonpolitician, meaning someone who hasn't served in any of the offices that form part of our constitutional republic. God wanted someone who wasn't afraid to preserve the values and traditions that made this country great. If Trump hadn't won, America would have been at risk of becoming more like Europe, and our freedoms would have been threatened. But the prayers of the righteous prevailed. You may say this is nonsense. Well, look at how the opposition has treated the president and how his supporters are attacked physically and told they cannot eat in certain restaurants. Look at the chaos the left has caused in the aftermath of George Floyd's death. Look at what has happened to the press.

190

Who could have imagined that the press in other nations would be freer and more responsible that some of the main television stations and printed press in America today? This country was not born to usurp its traditions just to become more accepted in the world. The world followed America, not the other way around. In the physical, as compared to Obama, Trump did not appear "presidential," but Trump has accomplished more in three years than any of his predecessors did in the same amount of time. But the press have hidden this from the American people. They have formed a cabal to prevent his re-election because they can't stand the president. I understand, and this is no big deal, although it is unfortunate. As free citizens of America, they have a right to their own opinion about who should become the next president of America. Nevertheless, as seasoned news anchor men and women, they have a moral obligation to provide independent, informative, and unbiased news to the world rather than repeating untrue narratives and hiding critical information from the American public in order to sway the elections. In a nutshell, they have overtly thrown their support to President Trump's opponent, who, during the few times he has appeared on television, is unfortunately showing signs of having a limited form of dementia.

Ironically, this, too, is hidden by the main press. I am praying the honorable former Vice President Joe Biden's cognitive intelligence is restored and that he is healed miraculously by the grace of God. I take no joy at all in seeing anyone go through what Vice President Biden is going through right now. The conservative news media and talk radio should stop making fun of him, and the liberal media should stop covering it up. Should he emerge victorious in 2020, Biden's vice president will be the most powerful vice president in our country's history since Vice President Dick Cheney of Wyoming, who held that position from 2000 to 2008 during the presidency of former President George Bush.

This woman would be the one running the show during a Biden presidency. I believe the American people deserve to know this so they can factor this truth into their decision making at the polls in November. This shouldn't be hidden from them, or it could cause problems in the future for our country. Before any debate takes place between Biden and Trump in September, nearly eight million Americans will have already voted through mail ballots.

Now, President Trump, in many ways, tends to take things too personally and can be impulsive at times, and this has unfortunately affected his approval rating as president. Yet he was raised to obey the directions of Elohim Chayim, and that was good enough for God, so God blessed his first term in office. The record low unemployment in the black community, the Hispanic community, and even in the Indian reservations is mind boggling. Prior to the Coronavirus pandemic, America was at its best both economically and militarily. We were poised for a great summer, and then, out of nowhere, China released a "late Christmas Gift" from Satan to the whole world after first opening the package. A little sense of humor about a terrible event. Secondly, no presidents had forcefully negotiated with China to reduce our deficit with them in the way that Trump did. It has to be part of the strategy to return America to a robust economy.

President Trump may not be aware of how much he is blessed to have a vice president who is a truly reborn. From what I discern from the spiritual realm, Pence is always praying for President Trump. Mike Pence is a gifted, inspirational orator, and he's very polished and clean. He is not perfect, yet he allows his fear of God to guide his everyday decisions in the best way he humanly can. Without any doubt, I will be the first to say President Trump has made many goofs that he could have avoided if he had just chosen to follow a specific Bible teaching, specifically where it says in the book of James to be slow to speak and quick to listen. President Obama mastered the gift of tempering

192

his speech, but President Obama, in my own opinion, did not fully grasp that America was strategically positioned by God to become what it is today. Yes, we've made some costly mistakes that our children's children will be paying for, such as the invasion of Iraq. Many nations in the world knew that Iran was far more able to build nuclear weapons at the time we invaded Iraq. Wolfowitz, Cheney, and Rumsfeld made a strategic mistake in targeting Iraq instead of Iran.

President Trump should ask the Holy Spirit for guidance each time he says anything publicly. I believe, without a doubt, that the former White House Press Secretary Sarah Huckabee never walked into the press briefing room without saying a short prayer, as she understood she was entering into a lion's den each time she addressed the press. A short prayer ensures a smooth delivery and avoids any unnecessary embarrassment. Nevertheless, like King Cyrus, Trump's enemies will never prevail over him because the hand of God is on Trump for reasons not yet revealed to the world. This hand isn't guaranteed if President Trump operates outside God's will. So I continue to pray for President Trump. In the past I knew that the Mueller investigation of President Trump would come to nothing, and it indeed came crashing down from the very beginning. Even worse for the opposition, it boomeranged to them. This outcome was revealed to me by God because the motive behind the investigation was eerie, evil, wrong, deceptive, and unacceptable in the eyes of God. Even worse, the deception that was propagated with cooperation of the mainstream media have torn this country apart, and they are unrepentant. Many people in the world are unaware that there is still a God in heaven that sees and reveals. I am waiting for the Durham report to unravel whether this was truly a plot to unseat an elected president. I know what was revealed to me, but I want to see what the Durham report will reveal to the American people.

There were some prophetic acts throughout the United States that brought Trump in. Billy Graham's son, Franklin Graham, who is now president of the Billy Graham ministry, agreed to obey God and go to every state in the nation to preach the gospel of repentance and salvation. I believe he usually preached in the state capital (political power) in each state. The size of the crowds depended on the states he went to. That act of obedience ensured we would get a person we were not even considering in office. I am shocked and indeed saddened that Senator Diane Feinstein of California and Senator Chuck Schumer, two powerful political people who are Jewish and understand the teachings of the Torah and the first five books of Moses, did not warn President Obama about what happens to nations that turn away from God and His principles only to engage in the things God hates. They know the truth, but they put their political party's doctrines and agendas ahead of the desires of the powerful God. Senator Feinstein and Senator Schumer, love America; they are patriots despite their disagreements with President Trump. You may ask what the big deal is. Israel has had more liberal laws than the United States, and they expanded their marriage laws before America, even allowing gays and lesbians in the military fifteen years before the United States did. This is all true, but Israel is not the United States. God made the United States the most powerful country militarily, economically, and politically, not Israel.

Our current president understands his purpose in life, and he knows his rise to power was nothing short of a miracle. Despite his shortcoming, President Trump, by all accounts, has been a friend of God's people globally, and he's an ardent supporter of the freedom of all religion. He has been a breath of fresh air in terms of identifying with the things of God, praying at cabinet meetings, and calling for the nation to pray when there is a national crisis. It is rare to find leaders in the 21st century who are bold in

194

identifying with the Christian way of life even though their countries have benefitted tremendously from its principle and commandments. Trump understands that most of the founding fathers of the United States of America entered into a covenant with God and that this is the single reason why America became a great nation.

It is God and only God who makes nations rise and fall. The good news for America is that the current leaders in China are indeed clueless about this truth while they continue to persecute Christians, incarcerate Muslims needlessly for their faith, and crack down on religious freedom. They think and believe they can accomplish what America has through their own human efforts. They are a very materialistic society with an avid hatred for religion, yet there are 100 million reborn Chinese. They want to become great and surpass America while cracking down on the Christian faith. What a big joke. They are swimming in a pool of utter confusion. It will only happen if America strays from the ways of God and begins to persecute Christians in the same way the Chinese do.

I also have a very strong word for Prime Minister Modi of India, whom I like and admire. A war on Christians in India will undermine the growing prosperity in India and undermine the advanced strides India is making as millions of people strive to enter into the middle class. The cry of the righteous against unjust persecution will provoke the anger of God against the predominantly Hindu nation. Study the history of nations and God's hand in their affairs carefully. America is still standing tall today despite its increasing proclivity to turn away from the things of God. This is because God is a covenant-keeping God. Equally important, there are still prophets, pastors, and minsters of the gospel, along with a fearless president, who are still calling on His name and interceding for this nation.

Grace allows us plenty of time (years for a nation) to enter into a spirit of repentance, therefore withholding

God's wrath against that nation collectively until its cup of iniquity is full. Just because a nation allows its citizen to do certain things based on the law of the land, it doesn't necessarily mean it is right in God's eyes. Senator Diane Feinstein and Senator Chuck Schumer, whom I respect, are not just senior senators in our nation's capital; they have also gained tremendous power in the United States Senate. They are of the Jewish stock, and thus they know the history of Israel, dating back nearly 5,000 years ago. They know what happened to Israel when they sacrificed their children to the god of Molech the Canaanite god), and they know how Elohim Chayim hated this detestable act and severely punished Israel. Are all these things not written in the five books of Moses and other parts of the Bible (Leviticus 20:3-5, 2 King 23:10, and in the book of Jeremiah)? God hates oppression of the poor, but He deals with this problem fundamentally differently than the way He deals with human sacrifice. This is what God said through the vocal chords of His prophet Jeremiah.

It is written: "They set up their abominations in the house, which is called by my name, to defile it. And they built places of Baal, which are in the valley of the son of Hinnom, to cause their sons and daughters to pass through the fire unto Molech; which I commanded them not, that they should do this abomination, to cause Judah to sin" (Jer 32:34-35 KJV).

There are about 195 countries in the world. Only twenty-six countries in the whole world have populations that are more than fifty-two million. I am sad to report to the American people that we have aborted around sixty-two million babies since Roe vs. Wade. We are competing with China in this act that causes heaven to frown on us. The blood that has been shed is crying out for vengeance, just like Abel's blood did. Even if you are pro-choice, is almost sixty-two million not enough? Spiritually, it empowers the kingdom of darkness in America. This allows Satan to then

196

use his unwitting human proxies and unleash things like mass shootings, terrorism, child rape and sexual exploitation, unwinnable wars that cost billions, economic decline, family division, children in rebellion against authority figures, lawlessness, and, worst of all, division among our citizens. Critical decisions we make on Earth affect whether we will receive blessings or curses in America.

Remember again that Satan's power over nations is limited to what we ourselves give to him. He cannot afflict a nation without God's permission, and God will not allow him unless we have violated and, for a long period, disobeyed God's laws. It is not too late to call upon God as a nation, and hopefully, such an outpouring will come forth this year because of the Lord's mercy on America. We are all waiting for a spiritual revival. When President Obama was running in a hotly contested primary with Madam Secretary Clinton in 2008, he said something like this: "We cannot, as a society, ignore the moral implications of abortion on demand." I agreed with the former president then. He hasn't said much since then. Democrats and Republicans, let us work together to prevent our country from shedding more blood and provoking the anger of God against a nation He Himself made so great.

Let Us Pray

EL Channun, our gracious God, it is written in Your Word that the earth is the Lord's. You laid the foundations of the earth on the seas and established it on the rivers. You are a very powerful God, and all other gods are the works of men. Now, grant us strength in the name of Jesus to recover fully from the Coronavirus. Empower us, as a nation, to overcome temptations that would cause us to depart from Your ways and the written Word of God. Raise up godly men and women of integrity from both political parties, and place them in the corridors of power in Washington

197

and in the state capitals. Help them fearlessly anchor our country to the covenant You had with the framers of our Constitution. Empower our leaders, regardless of their political affiliations, to stand up courageously for what is right and what is just in the eyes of You rather than what is popular and out of the will of God. Give us a new heart of flesh and write Your laws in our minds so that we may have a heart of repentance and turn from our wicked ways as a nation, lest Your anger burn against us, as it was with Israel several thousand years ago. May Your goodness and mercy follow us all the days of our lives so that we may dwell in the house of the Lord forever and ever. In Your Son's name. Amen.

Chapter 8

HE WHO OVERCOMES

The book of Revelation in the Bible is the only book that specifically says whoever reads it is blessed. Yes, God confers a blessing on all who read it, hear it, and heed what it says, taking everything to heart, for the time is at hand. (Things are about to happen soon that will signal things being wrapping up on the earth.) This book is a little more complex, for lack of a better word, than the other books that form the Bible. The things John, the disciple of Jesus Christ, wrote in the book of Revelation weren't written in a chronological order. This is very important because once you know this, it will help clear up any confusion you may have while reading. In the book of Revelation, certain things that occurred before the creation of man will be mentioned, but it will be in the middle of the twenty-two chapters rather than at the beginning. It is important to keep this piece of information in your mind when reading it. Nevertheless, it is a riveting account of things that already occurred, things that are occurring right now, and things that are to come. The book of Revelation is based on the visions John had while he was imprisoned on the island of Patmos, which is in modern-day Turkey, for sharing the gospel and the testimony of Jesus Christ. This took place when the other eleven disciples were already dead. They had been executed one after the other for the spreading of the gospel. Judas, one of the disciples, killed himself because he betrayed

Jesus, and he did not know how to repent, instead choosing to hang himself. The spirit of pride and the spirit of murder are the engines of any suicide on Earth.

The title of this chapter gives you a clear hint that there is a reward for he who overcomes. The question to you the reader is this: Overcome what? The goal of this chapter is to answer that question, and it is based on the first three chapters of Revelation. There are gifts God bestows on all saints (Christians, followers of Christ) who can overcome the temptations, trials, persecution, and intimidation caused by the devil. There is a great reward when you resist the temptation to follow the crowd on anything that is anathema and incongruous with biblical teachings and the Word of God. This reward lasts for eternity when you remain steadfast and unbendable, always obeying God rather than man, especially when you choose to stand against the world's views. It is not easy, and you will sometimes be ostracized by society. Jesus calls for patience on the part of the saints (reborn Christians). Many Christians today will give up as the persecution starts and will renounce their allegiance to Jesus Christ. For some, the trials will cause them to love less and hate more. Before Christ returns, Christians are going to be persecuted by all nations on the earth. Jesus Christ warned us about this in the gospel. Brothers and sisters will betray one another.

On the Lord's day, also known as sabbath, John had a vision and was caught up in the heavenly realm. Jesus appeared to John in a glorified body that John, who was close to Jesus, did not recognize. The Shekinah Glory — the indescribable, majestic, splendid appearance of Jesus Christ — was blinding because of its brilliance and brightness. Jesus had seven stars in His right hand, and He stood in the middle of seven golden lampstands. John fell to the ground and literally fainted in fright. Jesus touched him gently, which strengthened him, and then lovingly introduced

200

Himself. This was a strategic mission, and Jesus began to talk to John, who could barely stand.

It is written: "When I saw Him, I fell at His Feet as though dead. And He placed His right hand on me and said, 'Do not be afraid; I am the First and the Last [absolute Deity, the Son of God], and the Ever-living One [living in and beyond all time and space]. I died, but see, I am alive forevermore, and I have the keys of [absolute control and victory over] death and Hades (the realm of the dead). So write the things which you have seen [in the vision], and the things which are [now happening], and the things which will take place after these things. As for the mystery of the seven stars which you saw in My right hand, and the seven golden lampstands: the seven stars are the angels (divine messengers) of the seven churches, and the seven lampstands are the seven churches'" (Rv 1:17-20 AMP).

Keep in mind that a church in the eyes of Jesus is when two or three are gathered in His name. Again, not being part of a church does not make you exempt from the things Jesus told John through the angels of the seven churches, namely Ephesus, Smyrna, Pergamum, Thyatira, Sardis, Philadelphia, and Laodicea.

The mission of Jesus Christ in this vision was to convey His praise and constructive criticism to the seven different types of churches in Asia. In a nutshell, Jesus had come to highlight the things each of these seven churches were doing, whether they were in line with God's will or out of God's will. Now, none of these churches exist today. That said, the spirit in which they operated—what was taking place in those churches and how they ran their ministries— can be found in churches throughout the world today. This message is for everyone who identifies with Christ and belongs to a church today. It is also for anyone who doesn't necessarily belong to a church body but identifies as a Christian. And quite frankly, it is indeed for those who believe in other religions. I hope they will seek the face of the one true God before it is too late. The first three chapters of the book of Revelation speak of the churches of the past, but the messages are also relevant to the churches of today. It is also for anyone who sees himself or herself in the description Jesus gives when referring to the good and bad things the churches were doing. This message is also for people who attend various denominations of churches. When you ask them, "How do you know you are going to go to heaven," the first thing they do is start talking about themselves and what they have done to earn their way into heaven. Others stare at you and say, "I don't know." The latter pages in the book of Revelation are still for the Church, but they provide more of a warning to the unbelievers and those who are depending on their own human efforts to make it to heaven. This, for sure, would be a fruitless exercise in futility. Peter said in the book of Acts that there is no other name given to man under heaven by which one may obtain salvation. Only through Jesus Christ may it be obtained.

I have been asking myself, why did Jesus decide to send this very important message to the body of Christ at that time? It was as important then, as it is now important to the churches all over the world. The only answer that came to my spirt was this: Judgement will first begin in the house of God. He came to this earth as the Savior of the world, and He is returning as Judge of all mankind. Before Christ returns, even the churches must clean up their act. No exceptions. When they do, the rewards will be for eternity. Many pastors, preachers, and ministers of the gospel have preached on the book of Revelation. I have learned some important truths about this book. If you are not familiar with it, I highly recommend three pastors who will help you learn: Pastor Robert Morris of Gateway Church, Pastor Dr. Robert Jeffress of the Dallas Baptist Church, and, equally important, Irvin Baxter, who is the founder and president of the Endtime Ministries and is a seasoned prophet. His magazines go to various institutions in our country, including the State Department, the White House, and other national security agencies.

All of these men of God reside in the great state of Texas. Yee-haw! I highly recommend going to the website of their ministries and looking for their messages on the book of Revelation. More importantly, read it for yourself. I wrote this book primarily for the people of the world who have not yet come to the knowledge of the truth: that Jesus Christ had died for their sins so they could be reconciled with God when they depart from the earth by death or by rapture. I also wrote it for the Christian so that they will discover their purpose and not face the wrath of Jesus Christ, who, in the book of Luke, said, "...the master of that servant will come on a day when he does not expect him and at an hour he does not know, and will cut him in pieces, and assign him a place with the unbelievers" (Lk 12:46 AMP). I tremble myself as I write this book. Well, what does the Bible say? It says each one of us must work out our salvation with fear and trembling. The seven great rewards are worth it. There is nothing on Earth that can match any one of these rewards, because they are for eternity.

To the church in Ephesus, John wrote that Jesus was aware of their efforts, their suffering, and their patient endurance. He also commended them for having little tolerance for evil and those who engaged in evil practices. He appreciated their discernment when it came to identifying people who called themselves apostles but were imposters and liars. Jesus understood their suffering as they stood up for His name and the truth. (Remember that so many people of today are questioning the teachings of the Bible and saying man wrote it. They ignore the fact that those men wrote the Bible based on what God told them to write). On the critical side, the angel of the church in Ephesus conveyed Jesus' message that the church of Ephesus (or anyone who fits into this profile) had abandoned being on fire for God. He wanted them to start being on fire again for God.

The Word says, "But I have *this* [charge] against you, that you have left your first love [you have lost the depth of love that you first had for Me]. So remember *the heights* from which you have fallen, and repent [change your inner self— your old way of thinking, your sinful behavior—seek God's will] and do the works you did at first [when you first knew Me]; otherwise, I will visit you and remove your lampstand (the church, its impact) from its place—unless you repent" (Rv 2:4-5 AMP).

Jesus went back to applauding them for their deep hatred of the corrupt teachings of the Nicolaitans, because it misled people.

It is written: "Yet you have this [to your credit], that you hate the works *and* corrupt teachings of the Nicolaitans [that mislead and delude the people], which I also hate" (Rv 2:6 AMP).

So, who are the Nicolaitans today? They were a group of people who mixed the teachings of the Bible with the occult. They had no problem having one leg in the body of Christ and another leg in the occult as they worshiped other gods. They were working both sides and taught people that it was okay to do that. It is like practicing witchcraft and, at the same time, attending church. These are compromised Christians, and you cannot even tell the difference between them and unbelievers when they are outside a church setting. The pressure to feel accepted by your peers can make one indulge in sinful practices Jesus frowns upon. You can't act a certain way with your unbelieving friends and then act like a Christian on Sundays.

It is written: "He who has an ear, let him hear *and* heed what the Spirit says to the churches. To him who overcomes [the world through believing that Jesus is the Son of God], I will grant [the privilege] to eat [the fruit] from the tree of life, which is in the Paradise of God'" (Rv 2:7 AMP).

Saints, the tree of life is the tree that Adam and Eve missed because they were deceived by Satan, and they instead went to the tree of the knowledge of good and evil. This gift called the fruit of the tree of life is so important and great that when Adam and Eve realized they had sinned against God, although not mentioned in the Bible, they considered eating from this tree.

It is written: "And the Lord God said, Behold, the man is become as one of us, to know good and evil: and now, lest he put forth his hand, and take also of the tree of life, and eat, and live for ever..." (Gn 3:22 KJV).

But God deployed flaming swords and Cherubim to make sure Adam and Eve could never get to that tree of life, let alone re-enter the Garden of Eden. Now, if you are victorious—and Jesus is hoping you will be victorious—and you are able to overcome temptations, He has an awesome gift for you, one that is for eternity. This is the first great reward, apart from your salvation. I believe this reward, since it is coming from Jesus, will be greater than anything of material significance that one could receive on Earth. To the Church of Smyrna, Jesus referred to Himself as the First and the Last, who died and came to life. Jesus said He understood their suffering and poverty, but Jesus told them, "You are rich," which meant their decision to stand with Christ had a great reward in heaven, even though on Earth they were poor.

"I know thy works, and tribulation, and poverty, (but thou art rich) and I know the blasphemy of them which say they are Jews, and are not, but are the synagogue of Satan. Fear none of those things which thou shalt suffer: behold, the devil shall cast some of you into prison, that ye may be tried; and ye shall have tribulation ten days: be thou faithful unto death, and I will give thee a crown of life. He that hath an ear, let him hear what the Spirit saith unto the churches; He that overcometh shall not be hurt of the second death" (Rv 2:10-11 KJV).

Being of the synagogue of Satan meant they were Jews only by blood, and according to the amplified Bible, they did not believe in or truly honor the God they claimed to worship. In this particular church, those who stuck with Christ would end up becoming martyrs for God's Kingdom, but Jesus promised them a crown of life and told them they would not experience the second death, which is the lake of fire. This meant their names were in the Lamb's Book of Life, and they would not experience eternal separation from God. They would be part of the first resurrection.

It is written: "Blessed and holy is he that hath part in the first resurrection: on such the second death hath no power, but they shall be priests of God and of Christ, and shall reign with him a thousand years" (Rv 20:6 KJV). For further study, see verses four through six of chapter nineteen of Revelation. This is the second great reward that would last for eternity.

To the church of Pergamum, Jesus began by describing Himself to the angel of that church as the one who had the sharp, two-edged sword in his mouth.

The Word says, "'I know where you dwell, [a place] where Satan sits enthroned. Yet you are holding fast to My name, and you did not deny My faith even in the days of Antipas, My witness, My faithful one, who was killed (martyred) among you, where Satan dwells. But I have a few things against you, because you have there some [among you] who are holding to the [corrupt] teaching of Balaam, who taught Balak to put a stumbling block before the sons of Israel, [enticing them] to eat things that had been sacrificed to idols and to commit [acts of sexual] immorality. You also have some who in the same way are holding to the teaching of the Nicolaitans. Therefore repent [change your inner self—your old way of thinking, your sinful behavior— seek God's will]; or else I am coming to you quickly, and I will make war *and* fight against them with the sword of My mouth [in judgment]. He who has an ear, let him hear *and* heed what the Spirit says to the churches. To him who overcomes [the world through believing that Jesus is the

206

Son of God], to him I will give [the privilege of eating] *some* of the hidden manna, and I will give him a white stone with a new name engraved on the stone which no one knows except the one who receives it'" (Rv 2:13-17 AMP).

This is the third gift that lasts for eternity. The Bible refers to sexual immorality as any sexual encounter outside marriage, and this includes sex before marriage, which is now popular globally. Nevertheless, it is described as sin in God's eyes, as He invented sex and therefore has the right to set the rules on how it should be done. It takes God's grace to overcome this sin if you are still clinging to the things of this world and are not reborn. Many people who call themselves Christians, and those who simply attend church, are in sin because they live together while they are not married. The consequences of this disobedience have been devastating to the whole world, especially America. This sin isn't new. The woman in Samaria, also known as the woman at the well, was living with someone she wasn't married to when she met Jesus, but Jesus was delighted to meet her. Do not fill condemned, but know that you know the truth and should rectify your situation while there is time. The greater the challenges, trials, and temptations, the greater the reward. See what the church of Pergamum had to overcome, and their reward.

The Word says, "And unto the angel of the church in Thyatira write; These things saith the Son of God, who hath his eyes like unto a flame of fire, and his feet are like fine brass; I know thy works, and charity, and service, and faith, and thy patience, and thy works, and the last to be more than the first. Notwithstanding I have a few things against thee, because thou sufferest that woman Jezebel, which calleth herself a prophetess, to teach and to seduce my servants to commit fornication, and to eat things sacrificed unto idols. And I gave her space to repent of her fornication; and she repented not. Behold, I will cast her into a bed, and them that commit adultery with her into great tribulation, except they repent of their deeds. And I will kill her children with death; and all the churches shall know that I am he which searcheth the reins and hearts: and I will give unto every one of you according to your works. But unto you I say, and unto the rest in Thyatira, as many as have not this doctrine, and which have not known the depths of Satan, as they speak; I will put upon you none other burden. But that which ye have already hold fast till I come. And he that overcometh, and keepeth my works unto the end, to him will I give power over the nations: And he shall rule them with a rod of iron; as the vessels of a potter shall they be broken to shivers: even as I received of my Father. And I will give him the morning star," (Rv 2:18-28 KJV).

Similar to this story, several churches are beginning to tolerate rather than prohibit sexual immorality. One sin can gravitate to another if you are not on guard and vigilant. Sexual immorality is very contagious because it uses its most powerful component, called lust, to lure you into it. Once lust has taken its root in the bottom of your belly, you will need deliverance and meditation on the Word of God daily in order to get it out. This sin is rampant in many churches, and even certain pastors are involved in it with their congregation members.

There are many members of churches who go out and get "laid" on Saturdays, then come to church to sing "glory, hallelujah" on Sundays. Jesus is calling on them to abandon their ways and this lifestyle, or He will send them into great tribulation. Which means they could miss the rapture and go through the tribulation that is supposed to come on unbelievers and those who have the mark of the beast. He is willing to help because he loves them. I believe the people who are facing these challenges, if they can overcome such great trials, will indeed occupy a ruling position in the thousand-year reign with Christ and beyond. Remember, when Daniel was able to interpret King Nebuchadnezzar's dream, he got a position that put him in charge of several

208

provinces (nations that represented the empire of King Nebuchadnezzar), and he was literally second in command to King Nebuchadnezzar. Those who overcome will receive the morning star. One of Jesus' names is the Morning Star. This is the fourth great reward, which will last for eternity.

Now, this is what Jesus said to the angel of the Lord in the church of Sardis, and John wrote: "'To the angel (divine messenger) of the church in Sardis write: "These are the words of Him who has the seven Spirits of God and the seven stars: 'I know your deeds; you have a name (reputation) that you are alive, but [in reality] you are dead. Wake up, and strengthen *and* reaffirm what remains [of your faithful commitment to Me], which is about to die; for I have not found [any of] your deeds completed in the sight of My God *or* meeting His requirements. So remember *and* take to heart the lessons you have received and heard. Keep *and* obey them, and repent [change your sinful way of thinking, and demonstrate your repentance with new behavior that proves a conscious decision to turn away from sin]. So then, if you do not wake up, I will come like a thief, and you will not know at what hour I will come to you. But you [still] have a few people in Sardis who have not soiled their clothes [that is, contaminated their character and personal integrity with sin]; and they will walk with Me [dressed] in white, because they are worthy (righteous). He who overcomes [the world through believing that Jesus is the Son of God] will accordingly be dressed in white clothing; and I will never blot out his name from the Book of Life, and I will confess *and* openly acknowledge his name before My Father and before His angels [saying that he is one of Mine].'"'" (Rv 3:1-5 AMP).

In the further chapters of the book of Revelation, one can observe that the people in the church of Sardis, if they overcame and were victorious against sin, became part of the saints in heaven, who will join Jesus when He returns to the earth to defeat the antichrist.

It is written: "And I saw heaven opened, and behold, a white horse, and He who was riding it is called Faithful and True (trustworthy, loyal, incorruptible, steady), and in righteousness He judges and wages war [on the rebellious nations]. His eyes are a flame of fire, and on His head are many royal crowns; and He has a name inscribed [on Him] which no one knows *or* understands except Himself. He is dressed in a robe dipped in blood, and His name is called the Word of God. And the armies of heaven, dressed in fine linen, [dazzling] white and clean, followed Him on white horses" (Rv 19:11-14 AMP).

The fifth reward is for people who finally show some fruit worthy of their calling. This reward is for saints who have completed something instead of starting things and never finishing them—saints who have glorified the name of God by what they have done on Earth. They have stopped moving from church to church, carrying a critical spirit wherever they go. They have indeed made up their minds to be centered and grounded, to grow in the things of God, and to do something with the gifts God has given them. They have changed the way they think about themselves and stopped dwelling on sinful thoughts. In addition, they have changed their behavior to show that they have truly repented and turned from a lifestyle of sin.

Then Jesus spoke to the angel in charge of the church of Philadelphia, and John wrote the following: "...These things saith he that is holy, he that is true, he that hath the key of David, he that openeth, and no man shutteth; and shutteth, and no man openeth; I know thy works: behold, I have set before thee an open door, and no man can shut it: for thou hast a little strength, and hast kept my word, and hast not denied my name. Behold, I will make them of the synagogue of Satan, which say they are Jews, and are not, but do lie; behold, I will make them to come and worship before thy feet, and to know that I have loved thee. Because thou hast kept the word of my patience, I also will keep

210

thee from the hour of temptation, which shall come upon all the world, to try them that dwell upon the earth. Behold, I come quickly: hold that fast which thou hast, that no man take thy crown. Him that overcometh will I make a pillar in the temple of my God, and he shall go no more out: and I will write upon him the name of my God, and the name of the city of my God, which is new Jerusalem, which cometh down out of heaven from my God: and I will write upon him my new name" (Rv 3:7-12 KJV).

Jesus ends this message the same way He did with the previous churches. "He that hath an ear, let him hear what the Spirit saith unto the churches" (Rv 2:29 KJV). Jesus was clearly pleased with this church. This was because this church had little strength but still stuck with the Word of God. God also promised to protect them from the temptations many other churches, Christians, and peoples of the world would face in order to test their fidelity to the things of God. The rewards were unique, and everyone who overcame was very close to God and wouldn't have to leave God's presence at all. This is indeed an awesome reward, and it's one you can receive, too, if you continue to worship, remain steadfast in prayer, and do not compromise your fidelity to Christ and His kingdom. Jehovah El Gomolah will handsomely reward you. And this is the sixth great reward.

Finally, John noted down what Jesus had informed the church in Laodicea. It was as follows: "'To the angel of the church in Laodicea write: These are the words of the Amen, the faithful and true witness, the ruler of God's creation. I know your deeds, that you are neither cold nor hot. I wish you were either one or the other! So, because you are lukewarm— neither hot nor cold—I am about to spit you out of my mouth. You say, "I am rich; I have acquired wealth and do not need a thing." But you do not realize that you are wretched, pitiful, poor, blind and naked. I counsel you to buy from me gold refined in the fire, so you can become rich; and white clothes to wear, so you can cover your shameful nakedness; and salve to put on your eyes, so you can see. Those whom I love I rebuke and discipline. So be earnest and repent. Here I am! I stand at the door and knock. If anyone hears my voice and opens the door, I will come in and eat with that person, and they with me. To the one who is victorious, I will give the right to sit with me on my throne, just as I was victorious and sat down with my Father on his throne. Whoever has ears, let them hear what the Spirit says to the churches'" (Rv 3:14-22 NIV).

This is the seventh great gift that will last for all eternity. The number seven represents completion. The trials here were almost self-inflicted. Jesus expressed his frustration with people who fit this category because they could not make up their minds whether they were going to endure to the end or chicken out when the rubber met the road. They were married to the material world, and their wealth had unfortunately blinded them to the truth. Yet Jesus was willing to reveal Himself through the Holy Spirit to those who overcome. He made sure they would sit with Him on His throne. Jesus went so far to compare this great gift that would last for eternity to how He now sits at the right hand of His Father in heaven. Imagine being the right-hand man or woman of the Son of God and the Son of the highest. I would be ecstatic and filled with unspeakable joy. If you are rich and you haven't supported ministries preaching the gospel, now is the time. Put your money into a soul-winning church and learn about the things of God so that your "filthy garment" will be replaced with white linen and you will not miss the opportunity to enter into God's Kingdom in heaven.

Let Us Pray

Heavenly Father, I come to you in the name of Your only begotten Son, Jesus Christ. I praise your great and powerful name because there is no God like You. From the rising to the setting of the sun, Your name, O Lord, is glorified. I thank you for encouraging me to press on in order to fulfill the high calling You have for my life. I ask that You deploy the same angels on my behalf that were deployed and assigned to Jesus when He was in the garden of Gethsemane. Empower me from on high to complete Your perfect will for my life in Jesus' name. I need discipline and orderliness in my life in order to fulfill your perfect will, because you are a God of order. Jehovah El Ezer—the Lord, my Helper—thank You for answering my prayers. Oh, how great is Your goodness, which You have given to those who fear you. In Jesus' name I pray. Amen.

Chapter 9

KING JESUS: WHO IS HE?

He is the greatest figure in human history to have walked on the earth. He was born in Bethlehem according to the Word, which was written before He was born. There are forty-four distinct prophecies that were written in the Old Testament (Tanakh) of the Bible about Jesus before He was born. Nearly all of them have been fulfilled in the (Chadashah) New Testament of the Bible. There are no other gods or religions that have had this privilege of being spoken about before they arrived. Not Buddha. Not Mohammed. Not Ramakrishna. Not Shiva. Not Moses.

It is written: "But you, Bethlehem Ephrathah, though you are small among the clans of Judah, out of you will come for me one who will be ruler over Israel, whose origins are from of old, from ancient times" (Mi 5:2 NIV).

There is a huge, significant, undisputed difference between Jesus and all other religions deities that have come and gone. None of them had any books written about them before they were born, with the exception John the Baptist. Yes, predictions were made about world leaders in the Bible and other books before they arrived on the earth, but not other religious figures. He came into this world from a humble Jewish family. So let it be known today: Salvation started with the Jew, and it will end with the Jew. Salvation is of the Jew and from the Jew called Master Jesus.

214

It is written: "You Samaritans worship what you do not know; we worship what we do know, for salvation is from the Jews. Yet a time is coming and has now come when the true worshipers will worship the Father in the Spirit and in truth, for they are the kind of worshipers the Father seeks. God is spirit, and his worshipers must worship in the Spirit and in truth" (Jn 4:22-24 NIV).

Jesus spoke the words above to the woman in Samaria, known as the woman at the well. She had a divine encounter with Jesus, and once she found out that He was really who He said He was, she opened a mighty door for Jesus to preach the gospel about God's Kingdom and salvation in that city. This woman had been married five times and was living with another man she was not married to when Jesus met her. Yet He used her to save a whole city. God is not a respecter of persons. He would accept you as you are and then clean you up, and He would even use you in your rough state if you were willing to glorify His Father on the earth.

Jesus existed before the world was created. The Lord formed Him from the beginning (Prv 8), and He existed before the creation of the world. He rejoiced greatly in the Lord's handiwork as He fashioned the earth into its existence.

It is written: "'The Lord brought me forth as the first of his works, before his deeds of old. I was formed long ages ago, at the very beginning, when the world came to be. When there were no watery depths, I was given birth, when there were no springs overflowing with water; before the mountains were settled in place, before the hills, I was given birth, before he made the world or its fields or any of the dust of the earth. I was there when he set the heavens in place, when he marked out the horizon on the face of the deep, when he established the clouds above and fixed securely the fountains of the deep, when he gave the sea its boundary so the waters would not overstep his command,

and when he marked out the fountains of the earth. Then I was constantly at his side. I was filled with delight day after day, rejoicing always in his presence, rejoicing in his whole world and delighting in mankind" (Prv 8:22-31 NIV).

He is the only begotten Son of the Father, Hashem. He is in Elohim, and Elohim is in Him. He is part of the Trinity, known as God the Father, God the Son, and God the Holy Spirit. He is the one who sent the Holy Spirit to us. He is the light of the world. He is the light that shines in darkness, and darkness cannot comprehend it. He is the light that shines on all men who come unto the earth (Jn 1). He is the great overcomer of difficulties. He is the Savior of the world. He was the one who was slain before the creation of the world. He is the Word of God. For it is written, "In the beginning was the Word, and the Word was with God, and the Word was God" (Jn 1:1 KJV). He grew up as a tender shoot out of a dry ground, and there was nothing comely that we should take note of him or anything significant that we should adore him (Is 53). He came to atone for the sins of the world. He suffered egregiously for our sakes. He is the Lamb of God. He is the lion of the tribe of Judah. He bore the sins of the whole wide world and offered an invitation that tells you to believe in Him and to believe that He died for your sins, and then your eternal life is secured. You will be filled with joy unspeakable, and as soon as you leave this world, you will be with Him in paradise in Heaven. For to be absent in the flesh (death) is to be instantly in the presence of the Lord (immediate afterlife). Jesus is the bread of life. He who comes to Him will never be hungry, and he who believes in Him will never be thirsty. He rescues His people from great trials, and He is the fourth man in the fire (Dn 3:25).

He is the Messiah. He is the one Mary Magdalene cried out to when she realized Jesus had risen from the dead after she saw Him by the cave that held His empty tomb. She called him "Rabboni," meaning "Master. He is our Kinsley Redeemer. He is our burden bearer, our advocate, and all

216

authority has been given to Him in heaven and on Earth. He walked on water, defying gravity. He went through physical walls after His resurrection, letting His disciples know, see, and observe that He had risen from the dead and that He had a glorified body. His voice is like the waves of an ocean, the voice of many waters. He has hair white as wool, and His face is twelve times brighter than the noonday sun. His eyes are like blazing fire. His hands still carry the scars from the long nails that were hammed into His hands. He is the Way, the Truth, and the Life. No one comes to the Father except through Him.

He is Jehovah El Olam, the everlasting Father. He is the Prince of peace. He is the great high priest in the order of Melchizedek. He is the great I am that I am. He told the Pharisees and Sadducees He existed before Abraham. His loving kindness is better than life. He hears the cry of the righteous and delivers them from all their trouble. He is the vine and calls you His branch. He is the root and offspring of David and the root of Jesse. He is the wonderful counselor, mighty God, everlasting Father, and Prince of peace (Is 9:6). He is the one who holds the seven stars in his right hand, and He stands in the middle of seven golden lampstands (Rv 1). He is the alpha and omega, and He is the eternal rock of ages. He is the true prophet of God and the author and perfecter of our faith (Heb 12).

He is the God of all hope, and this hope does not disappoint at all, because God's love has been poured into our hearts by the Holy Spirit, which was given to us the moment we were reborn. Jesus is full of unfailing love, full of compassion, and full of mercy, and He the joy to the world. He does not want anyone to perish; instead, He wants us to have everlasting life. He is the resurrection and the life (Jn 11). He is the one whose garment was dipped in blood, and He will return with tens of tens of thousands of angels. He and His Father are one. If you have seen Him, you have seen the Father. He dwells in unapproachable light. He is the great shepherd of the sheep. He is our shepherd, and we are His sheep. He is the feet washer. He washed the feet of His disciples in a prophetic act to say their sins had been washed (Jn 15). He took twelve disciples who were rough around the edges and untrained. He molded them for His glory and then sent them to spread the gospel to the world. He is coming back to wipe out wickedness from the earth and to establish His Kingdom on Earth. Every other god will bow and worship Him. He is the greatest remolding agent in the heavens and on the earth. He will change you from what you are to what you should be if you have yet to discover your purpose in life. He is beyond time. Time has always been on His side, and He holds the keys of death and Hades (Rv 1:18). He is judge of all and head of all principality, powers, dominion, and rulers in this age and the eternal age to come (Eph 1:18-23).

HE IS ALL TOGETHER LOVELY, ALL TOGETHER BEAUTIFUL, AND FAIRER THAN 10,000 OF THEM ALL. HIS LOVING KINDNESS IS BETTER THAN LIFE. MY LIPS SHALL PRAISE HIS NAME.